I0063380

WINNING
MATCH

WINNING MATCH

LEADERSHIP
FOR GAME CHANGERS

Together Toward the Extraordinary

DR. CHRISTIAN MARCOLLI

Foreword by Severin Lüthi,
Longtime Coach of Tennis Legend Roger Federer

WINNING MATCH

Leadership for Game Changers

Together Toward the Extraordinary

First Edition

Copyright © 2025 by Dr. Christian Marcolli

Winning Match® is a registered trademark
of Marcolli Executive Excellence AG, Switzerland

Published by
Munn Avenue Press
300 Main Street, Ste 21
Madison, NJ 07940, USA
MunnAvenuePress.com

MUNN
AVENUE
PRESS

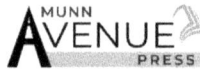

All rights reserved. No part of this publication
may be reproduced, distributed, or transmitted in any form
or by any means, including photocopying, recording,
or other electronic or mechanical methods, without the
prior written permission of the publisher and author,
except as permitted by U.S. copyright law.

For permission requests, contact MunnAvenuePress.com

Hardcover ISBN: 978-1-969679-04-9
Paperback ISBN: 978-1-969679-03-2
eBook ISBN: 978-1-969679-02-5
Audiobook ISBN: 978-1-969679-05-6

CONTENTS

"The true power of leadership
lies not only in reaching great results,
but in creating the conditions for
others to achieve the extraordinary."

– Dr. Christian Marcolli

FOREWORD

911 Matches prepared with Roger Federer.

226 Different opponents.

83% Success Rate: 755 wins and 156 losses.

10 Grand Slam Titles.

3 ATP World Tour Finals Titles.

55 ATP Tournament Titles.

1 Davis Cup Victory as the Swiss Davis Cup Captain.

1 Olympic Gold & 2 Olympic Silver Medals as the Head Coach of the Swiss Tennis Delegation at three Olympic Games.

This is the bottom line of my career as a professional tennis coach up to today.

—

Looking at these incredible numbers makes me grateful. And it gives me goosebumps. When I reflect on my journey, I still vividly remember the many moments of success, pride, and joy.

And I also remember the moments in my career when I had a scary realization: The stakes suddenly felt much higher in the work I was doing, and I wasn't sure if I had what it took to be successful. Ten years into my career as a professional tennis coach, I became the coach for the greatest player on the world stage at that time: legend and icon Roger Federer.

Roger had a unique rise to the top tier of professional tennis. We knew each other through the junior circuit in Switzerland, where I was also competing. Roger is only a few years younger than me. After my pro career as a player ended early, I started with some smaller coaching roles. This is when Roger and I reconnected. Roger brought me into his team first as his sparring partner, then as a part of his extended coaching staff, and ultimately, I rose to be his head coach in 2008. I had the privilege of coaching Roger until the end of his career. I will always remember his very emotional retirement from professional tennis in the O2 Arena in London.

The entire era when I was coaching Roger was incredible and very special. The early years were already very exciting, as Roger was performing at his peak, capturing title after title, including all Grand Slam victories, the Australian Open, the French Open, Wimbledon, the US Open, and winning the Olympic gold in doubles with Stan Wawrinka in Beijing.

Over the course of the many years at the top of the world of tennis, new and aggressive competitors were chasing his position, and sustaining that top position got harder and harder. Rafael Nadal and Novak Djokovic made it clear that they were here to stay and would stop at nothing to unseat Roger. The travel demands for a full competition schedule year after year were also intense, in addition to the tremendous demands of a global sports celebrity, which were a lot to sustain. In addition to maintaining a full training regimen, Roger's family was growing, and later in his career, he was fighting a battle with his own physical challenges, specifically some injuries that required adaptations to his game.

Through all of this, what was clear to me was this: If I couldn't deliver my absolute best as the coach, then Roger the player might fail. And I felt an enormous pressure to support him in the best way possible. There were moments when I was very confident and convinced about my strategies and tactics to implement. But there were also moments when I questioned my instincts, asking myself if I could be the kind of coach and leader that Roger needed me to be. However, in every moment, I fully committed myself to being the coach who will make the best — Roger — even better.

In most professional domains, at such moments, you can maybe get advice from an experienced person or mentor who has gone through all of this before themselves, and now can give you guidance for your new challenges. In our sport, however, there are only a few tennis coaches at the highest level, and naturally, they work for opposing players. So I had neither mentors nor peers that I could reach out to. And, in tennis, there is no playbook for coaches or anything like that for those at the very top. Therefore, over the years, I was regularly confronted with new, challenging, and unanticipated situations. As a result, I felt quite alone at times.

To be the strongest support to Roger, I needed somebody on my side who could help me untangle the complexities of my role and help me continue to grow and develop as a coach. Up to then, I felt that I had to know everything myself, and that I could not open up to anyone, as the general interest in Roger was extremely high, and I didn't want to risk anything leaking to the public. But I knew that this was potentially also standing in the way of my growth.

Then I crossed paths with Christian Marcolli, who I will call Chris going forward. Chris is one of the world's leading performance psychologists and leadership experts. As you can imagine, whenever you reach the top levels of any discipline, whether it is sports or business, the number of people you know is enormous, but the community of trusted friends and advisors can feel very small. Deep inside, I knew that I needed my own sparring partner, of course not on the court, but someone who I could exchange ideas with, who could challenge me, question me, inspire and motivate me, and provoke me with new ideas and perspectives.

Chris had himself been a professional footballer in Switzerland, and I learned during our first conversations that our life paths had taken similar twists and turns. Like me, he had a strong talent, a lot of passion, and a true love for sports already at a young age; in his case, it was football. He rose through the ranks in the Swiss football junior leagues, played for the Swiss Junior National Teams, and by age seventeen, had three professional contracts in hand, ultimately signing with the FC Basel, one of the biggest clubs in Switzerland. He played professionally for the club for a few years, but faced many challenges. They included careless leadership that served only the strongest egos on the team, pressure to succeed in direct competition with his teammates, and the expectation to perform well in an environment where teamwork and generosity were rarely rewarded. In this cutthroat performance context, Chris struggled to handle the pressure and had a hard time showing his full potential. He ultimately ended up in the hospital with career-ending knee injuries. I could fully relate to his story, having been through a similar rise and disappointments as a professional tennis player.

Chris knew what it meant to forge a new path, and like me, he also wasn't ready to walk away from the world of elite sports when his pro career as a player ended. Although he suffered great frustration from the medio-cre coaching he received, he had a strong conviction that there were other ways to unlock an individual's ability to reach their highest potential. He shifted to studying psy-chology, getting a doctorate, and performing academic research while establishing his coaching practice. Back then already, Chris didn't just work with elite professional athletes and sports stars, but also with Fortune 500 corpo-rations, executives, and leaders.

I knew that with his own background and story, Chris was familiar enough with my world to understand the intense environment and many of my daily challenges. In addition, Chris had some specific insights into my per-formance context since he had worked with Roger as his mental performance coach during an important period early in his career. That work helped Roger increase his mental toughness so he could perform well in the heat of the moment. The player you saw the most in his career—calm, playful, and centered—is also a result of Roger's desire to overcome that weakness and all the hard work he put in to get there.

I was eager to learn from Chris's experience coaching high performers and leaders across all disciplines, not just in elite sports but also from the world of business. I was seeking to even better understand the psychology of champions, so that I could create a shift in my own work and best support the most promising players I was working with, which included not just Roger, but also the National Tennis Team for Switzerland, the Swiss Davis Cup Team. I was immediately drawn to Chris's open style and how he was not just at the level of theory but had a deep and practical knowledge of the world of high performance in general. Most importantly, I knew that he was always in my corner, that when I needed support, he had my back. And I knew from Roger that Chris was a great guy to work with. It was very reassuring for me to have that exchange.

Throughout my career, I worked with Chris as my executive coach and leadership sparring partner for twelve years. And to this day, Chris is a valued advisor and friend, whom I consult regularly. Looking back, many of my career-defining moments, where I had to take a risk or build a new strategy, for example, how to win the Davis Cup, were also achieved thanks to the rigorous sparring I did with Chris. He always challenged me, pushed me, asked me the tough questions, and helped me unpack my own beliefs and fears. He engaged with me in a dialogue that was trusting, caring, thoughtful, and rigorous, and I left our sessions like I do at the end of a hard workout—feeling great, and with renewed energy and focus. I always left Chris full of new ideas and the confidence to make the changes I needed to make to be the right kind of leader for the players I was coaching. I draw upon our work together on a daily basis and feel that it has changed me and shown me a path to a different kind of leadership.

In this book, Chris shares not just his wisdom and experience, but also some research and insights from working with hundreds of leaders from some of the world's most recognized companies, as well as the world of elite sports. The Winning Match concept that Chris will introduce to you in this book certainly helped me become one of the top tennis coaches in the world. I have no doubt that reading this book will be game-changing for you. You will dive deep into what characterizes potential Game Changers, what makes them tick, and what sets them apart from the rest. And the most important thing that you will learn is how you can adapt your leadership to make your best people even better, together toward the extraordinary, in a true Winning Match.

Severin Lüthi
Longtime Coach of Tennis Legend Roger Federer

PROLOGUE:
Leadership for the Extraordinary

I am often asked, "How is it working with people who are among the best of the best in their fields? Do you need to interact with them differently?" Let me start with this: It is a great privilege when you get the chance to work with some of the absolute best of the best, the leaders and trendsetters in teams and organizations who are performing and delivering at the highest level in the worlds of business and elite sports. These individuals are creating the paths for innovation, setting the future direction, and shaping the world as we know it.

For more than two decades, as a performance coach to business leaders and elite athletes, I have spent my time in two very different worlds. In the world of elite sports, where some of my clients are among the world's most recognized athletes and players, and in the world of business, where I work with C-suite leaders of some of the world's most distinguished companies. When I compare these different arenas, the worlds at times could not feel more different. One day, I watched one of my clients win gold at the Olympic Games. The next day, I was on a call with a CEO right before he made a decisive presentation for the Fortune 500 company's board. The context often feels different, but the parallels between elite sports and the world of business draw upon most of the same principles of success.

This book is a collection of some of the key insights from my work as a psychologist and performance coach. I see every day what makes my diverse roster of clients truly different from the others. Although I most often work behind the scenes and, for the most part, stay largely invisible, the work I do with my clients is at close distance. The exchange is real, vulnerable, intense, focused, and goal-oriented. I have been up close when the athlete or business leader has completed the performance of a lifetime, remembering their fears and old patterns that once stood in the way, and knowing what it took for them to examine and adapt their approach to reach that next level and exceed their limits. It is especially gratifying because I know that it wasn't luck, or brute force, or an accident. Rather, strategic hard work and intensive sparring catalyzed and contributed to a critical shift in their thinking and behavior.

My insights and research make me ever more convinced that world-class is no coincidence. It's instead the result of many extremely specific interactions between top performers and top leadership. This, too, will become evident when you read this book. Through *Winning Match*, I am making this knowledge widely available for the first time for CEOs, business leaders, decision-makers, entrepreneurs, top managers, and innovators. In short, for all executives who are committed to making a difference with and through others. The views that I share, of course, are mine and therefore mostly subjective. They are founded on my personal experiences. But they are also shaped by the research I've done and the conclusions I've made based on my many years of working in the field of high performance. To make it more comprehensive and tangible for you, I will share not only key concepts but also various real-life examples to illustrate how these theories work in action. But to preserve my clients' confidentiality, the protagonists are composite characters, and their stories represent some of the most pressing issues and experiences in a reasonably anonymized, yet still realistic and concrete way.

Overall, it is a war for talent. Yes, you hear it often. Every company fights to recruit and land exceptional individuals because they persistently and reliably produce extraordinary results. We know them to be more committed and determined, more visionary and creative than their peers. They have the potential to innovate and take things to a new level with breakthrough ideas and perspectives. But it's unfortunately all too common for these outstanding individuals to fall short of their considerable potential when they are not paired with the necessary leadership. This is a massive risk and can have significant negative consequences. Some worst-case scenarios include when they leave the company for another organization with the promise of better, more supportive leadership. Or they become a direct competitor, founding their own company or launching a start-up.

I wrote this book to inspire you, to better enable you to scout and recognize your potential Game Changers, and to foster an environment with the necessary leadership competencies that will maximize their abilities to push boundaries and perform at their potential. In other words, I will show you what to look for to find the absolute best in a sea of talented individuals, and how to specifically interact with them so that the best get even better. In this fiercely competitive global marketplace, these abilities will give you a competitive advantage. I have experienced it time and again: Exceptional people with game-changer potential are fundamentally able to achieve great things. And they do exist in almost every company. But it is only when those exceptional individuals are connected with exceptional leadership that the enormous and ground-breaking game-changer potential can be unleashed.

The questions I now ask you: Do you know the people with game-changer potential in your organization? In a crowded team of high achievers, do you know the few that are not just very good, but have the potential to produce the exceptional, the game-changing? And if you identify and recognize these precious few, what do you do to help them achieve the extraordinary and pave the way for them to reach their best performance? Do you focus on your extraordinary people in extraordinary ways? Do you help them perform even better than you or they ever imagined?

When you can identify potential Game Changers and utilize specific leadership skills, strategies, and attitudes to elevate them to the top of their arena and allow their performance to make a true impact, then you are doing something rare and powerful: You are what I call a Leadership Champion. You join a cadre of elite and exceptional leaders who can unlock the greatness of the Game Changers in their teams and organizations, just as the best coaches in the world do with outstanding athletes in professional sports.

In the following chapters, I will share more about how outstanding excellence in your company is a deliberate result of when individuals with game-changer potential and Leadership Champions pair up in a specific way to form a **Winning Match**, driven by leadership that exceeds the ordinary and unlocks the extraordinary.

BUT FIRST, MY STORY

Yes, this book is based on my experience as a performance psychologist and coach to corporate leaders and elite athletes. But at the heart of it, this book ties deeply to my own experience as a professional footballer, and the journey I took to get there. Before I start, just a quick note for anyone more familiar with the term 'soccer': when I say 'football', that's the sport I am referring to.

So, let me start with my own story, which begins in a small village in northwestern Switzerland, in a very small town of around 500 people, where I was born. This is the neighboring village to the place where my mother was born. She was an only child, raised in a farming family with hardworking and traditional values. The people from this village tend to stay close to home, value family and tradition, and are strongly connected to their roots. That's the Swiss side of the family. My father, on the other hand, was the child of an Italian father who immigrated to Switzerland with his parents to get a job and hope for a better life. They ended up in the region of Basel. My Italian grandfather landed a job in industry and worked at a large chemical company. Eventually, he met and married my grandmother, who was a Basel native. In his spare time, he was a dedicated musician and conductor for a local orchestra. My father followed in similar footsteps. He acquired an education and a stable job at age sixteen in finance for a pharmaceutical company, one of the biggest companies in the region. He proudly clocked into this job until he retired earlier than planned at age sixty due to a company restructuring. My mother worked at home, raising us children. My parents shared the same values of hard work, stability, and tradition.

It may be needless to say, but having a professional footballer as a son didn't really fit into my parents' worldview. Football was a game, a way to pass the time, a hobby, not an actual career. If you asked my Italian grandfather, he would say that football was something for the working class, the "Volk". And, funny enough, as a working-class person himself, he aimed higher for his family. Therefore, my father was never really encouraged to play the game, although he kind of liked it. But when my father had children of his own, he spent quite a lot of his free time playing football with me and my older brother, which is how football entered my life. My dad taught me at first, then my parents signed me up for a local club at age six. All through primary school, I trained twice a week, a nice activity for an energetic kid like me.

But for me, two times a week wasn't enough. I wanted to play every day. I wanted to play all of the time. I loved the physicality of the game. I loved running, shooting, dribbling, learning, challenging myself, mastering footwork, and building up endurance. I watched football on TV whenever I could. Every afternoon after school, I would rally my friends to play with me. The best afternoons were those when we would play until dark. Some days, no one showed up. Nonetheless, I played on my own, drilling and dribbling around trees, always hoping that someone would join. Even then, I was driven by an insatiable desire to play, to master, and to get better.

My parents thankfully saw my passion for football and were impressed by my extreme focus. At the age of twelve, I trained under a coach who once played on the professional level. This was a very rare opportunity for countryside children. And right away, the coach saw my potential and later put my name forth for the regional selection team, Nordwestschweizer Auswahl. There, I played alongside top young junior talents from FC Basel, the big club in the nearby city. That became an important turning point.

It was when I went from being an unknown, countryside player to being among the best on a competitive team in a regional selection and suddenly getting the attention of scouts. By the time I was fourteen, I was scouted for various teams in the Swiss junior league, marking my first step on a path to the professional elite level.

This is where things got tricky for the first time. Up to that point, my parents were supportive, encouraging. They liked the lessons of hard work and discipline that I was getting from sports, and I was staying out of trouble. Overall, they admired the focus and dedication that this activity brought to my life. But they were also pragmatic. Sports were a hobby. School and academics were what mattered; they were priority number one, nonnegotiable.

But this new level of football had new demands. When I had the chance to join the FC Basel juniors, my parents shook their heads no. That would have meant more than a sixty-minute train and bus ride to the city every day for training, plus the same journey back at night. That would leave not enough time for schoolwork and family life. My parents declared that if I wanted to join a junior club, it would need to be closer to home, and I was allowed to participate only if there was no impact on my school grades.

Fortunately, I was a quick study. I liked school, and I had a good ability to focus and retain information. So, I didn't have a hard time juggling school and sports. The schoolwork came easily, and I could get good marks without a massive amount of effort. And of course, I had an important motivation to keep the grades up: I knew that was the only way I could continue playing football. My love for the game was so intense, so exciting, and encompassing; I started to dream of going pro. I could really see what that would take, and I was ready for it.

But my parents had entirely different aspirations for me. My mother's dream for me was a stable career and a regular paycheck, which would lead to a stable life. She imagined me staying close to home, working a job behind the bank counter in the next village. Her vision wasn't too far away from the path my father took. And that his father took. And less physically demanding than her father, who worked as a plasterer. Although my father supported me in a more unspoken way by driving me to the training sessions and matches whenever he could, and staying to watch me play, it felt like almost all of the important people in my life were saying: Enjoy the sport, have fun! But when it's time, get serious about your schoolwork and finding a real professional career path.

I, on the other hand, envisioned scoring the game-winning goal for Switzerland in the World Cup final against Argentina. It was my dream, and I visualized it almost daily.

It's kind of crazy when you think about it. Switzerland has never been in a World Cup final. Not even close. But hey, it's the truth; this was my vision.

As a result, there was a time when I resented my parents. I felt emotionally isolated in my ambition to play football at the highest level. The one thing I wanted most in life seemed like a betrayal to them, and it started to divide us. But I knew I had to carve my own path, even if it meant that I would stand somewhat in opposition to them and their vision for my future. We had occasional arguments, nothing too dramatic, but an undercurrent of tension in the house. I felt their skepticism, and they saw my determination to go my own way. When I look at it all now, from my standpoint as a father of two sons on the brink of adulthood, each discovering his own passions, I can fully understand where my parents were coming from. I can see clearly their fears and can see all that they felt was at risk. I get it deeply. Every parent wants their child to avoid disappointments and failure. Every parent wants their child to succeed and have a smooth and predictable path to success. They just didn't think that football was the best path, and they didn't want to support me in taking this risky option.

Yet despite their reservations, they didn't completely say no. And my father quietly continued to come to all of my games. So, instead of joining FC Basel, the compromise was that I played for FC Aesch, a lesser-known club that was closer to home and had a strong junior program. Aesch was a scrappy underdog team, with an amazing sense of camaraderie and can-do spirit. For three great years, I played at the highest junior level, in a fantastic and connected team, competing against powerhouse junior clubs like FC Basel and the Grasshopper Club Zurich. We defied everyone's expectations and had a great time doing it. And my parents were pleased that I managed to do it all while doing well with my academics.

During my time with this club, I was called up to play for the Swiss junior national team. I was ecstatic. I was so excited to represent my country and compete internationally against other junior national teams from Ireland, Norway, and Belgium. I got to wear the red jersey with the Swiss cross and sang our national anthem before the matches. I scored my first goal for Switzerland against Wales. We won three to two. It was incredible. A whole new level. And it put me firmly on the radar of the scouts for professional clubs.

At sixteen, I was invited to move out of the juniors to the first team at Aesch, to play alongside experienced men in the Swiss fourth division for the first time. The coach of the first team recognized my talent. However, initially, he held me back on the bench, which tested my patience and drive. I wanted to be out there playing and scoring, and I was so ready. When I finally got my chance, I went out on the pitch and scored immediately. In my third match, I netted four goals, which is unusual, especially for such a young player. It landed me in the local newspapers. I felt great. But my coach was tough. The day after those four goals, I waited for his pat on the back during training. But instead, he said, "Yes, four was all right. But you could have scored seven."

That moment changed me. He was right. I scored four goals but missed three other good chances. I became obsessed with pushing my limits from then on. I started to distinguish myself on the field, and professional clubs took notice. Grasshoppers Zurich, the reigning Swiss champions at the time and the most decorated club in the history of Swiss football, got in touch with me. Their sporting director, Erich Vogel, told my club, Aesch, that he was sending his scouting crew to my next game and that he would personally come to watch me play. My coach told me who was coming, but I think it would have been better if he kept that information for himself. Knowing that the recruiters were in the audience, I was full of nerves and totally in my head. I had a hard time keeping it together on the field and didn't play at my best, to say the least.

But despite my inconsistent performance on that day, I still managed to score a really nice goal.

After the match, Erich Vogel called me in the evening at my parents' home and said bluntly, "Christian, I have to be honest: You were terrible today. But that one goal you scored, well, there was something in it that only very few players have. And because of that, I want you." He invited me to train with the professional team, the then reigning Swiss champions, for two weeks in Zurich to get a better sense of my potential.

When I shared the news at home, I was ready to celebrate. My parents were not. This was a new step up, a more dangerous sign that this pro career could maybe actually happen. My mother, in particular, had the strongest negative reaction as I had two more years of school to complete: "You haven't even finished high school." "A football career could be short-lived and volatile." "Where was this fast train going?" "Who are these slick recruiters selling you dreams?" "If this doesn't work out, you will end up under the bridge." Both of my parents looked at this incredible opportunity through the lens of risk for failure. While I saw this as an opportunity to chase my dream, they saw danger, uncertainty, and peril. Nevertheless, at this important fork in the road, I wanted to charge ahead. But I felt deeply their hesitation and lack of confidence in the road ahead. Confronted with these omnipresent thoughts and emotions, I also started to have moments of doubt.

As much as I didn't want to rock the boat at home, I knew I had to do it. Despite my parents' resistance, I seized the opportunity and commuted daily to Zurich to train alongside national team players, the same ones who I had seen on TV. They were much older. They arrived in fancy sports cars. Yet I was determined to prove myself. I had stars in my eyes and fire in my heart. And I presented myself really well in these two weeks.

Ottmar Hitzfeld was the head coach of the Grasshopper Club Zurich at the time. He later moved on and became the head coach of world-class teams like FC Bayern Munich, winning the UEFA Champions League with two clubs, and was elected World Coach of the Year twice. After the training period, he called me up and told me that he was very impressed, that he sees something in me that is special, and that he wants me to join his team—now. I was not even eighteen years old. I was thrilled, to say the least. Consequently, the Grasshopper Club Zurich made me a formal offer to join their pro team. They wanted me to start right away.

As you can imagine, my parents weren't convinced, to say the least, especially since it was the middle of the school year: "How will you finish and get your diploma?" "You have two years to go until graduation!" they reminded me. I went back to the Grasshoppers' management. They thought I was crazy not to jump at the offer. So, they upped their offer with a better salary, promised a private tutor to keep me on track with schoolwork, presented a detailed plan for how they would further develop me as a player, and finally, after feeling my hesitation, guaranteed me playing time in every match in the remaining first season! It was an incredible offer, almost too good to be true, yet my parents were still skeptical. The financial terms were generous, and the contract promised financial stability for at least three years. But then what? I was convinced that it would be the right place for me, but my parents felt that I was too young to move away from home and the family support system.

Then FC Basel, a rival club, and at the time less top-ranked, stepped in with a competing offer that allowed me to finish school while continuing to live at my parents' home. On paper, it was the logical choice, the safe choice. This was my hometown club. The legendary club that I loved so much that I had their posters all over my room when I was a kid. The club where my father took me as a little boy to the stadium. The first ever football shirt I wore was from FC Basel. I felt torn. This was a dream come true. But deep down, I wasn't sure just how enthu-siastic they were for me to join. I didn't see their vision for my development as a player, and wondered if they just wanted to keep me away from the rival team. But the offer ticked some important boxes, certainly for my par-ents, and everyone around me seemed happy with it. So, I told myself that it was a reasonable compromise, even if I wasn't fully convinced. I accepted the offer. I was happy to know that I could continue pursuing my dream and still have the backing and support of my family. It was much more of a head decision than a heart decision, but I talked myself into it and was determined to make it work.

Joining FC Basel was a wild ride. Think of your home city, region, or country team, in any sport, and how much dedication that team gets from the fans. And now you are one of their players! I got to experience that excitement and adoration daily. There was the thrill of playing often in front of thousands of passionate fans calling out your name. The big stadium, the lights, the energy, and the media coverage. All of it was incredible. The prestige of driving a club-branded car and the special perks of being a local hero whose fans travel to see you play live. The din-ner at your favorite restaurant, but the bill is on the house. The free haircut and the complimentary drink or coffee.

People recognize you on the street and want to congratulate you. It was very special indeed.

But in the locker room, it was a whole other story. The team dynamics were cutthroat. Unlike Aesch, where camaraderie and joy fueled our performance, FC Basel's culture at that time was all about competition and ego. Veteran and more experienced players sought to protect their position, wanting to hang on to their contracts as long as possible and at all costs. This made younger players like me a threat. For the first time, I saw how the commercial aspects of the game undermined our team dynamic. When each goal netted a financial bonus for the one who kicked it into the net, there was less reason for any player to pass the ball, and all the more reason to fight with your teammate to be the one who scored.

I had learned the hard way that this was a completely new world. I was naive. I hoped someone would take me under their wing to help me develop my skills, or even just navigate the team dynamics. I had a strong desire to get input from the more experienced players and coaches so that I could make changes and perfect my game. But the environment was all about ego, status, glory, and survival—every man for himself. There was no one whom I felt I could trust, and few who took any interest in my success. Instead, the star forward, a charismatic but ruthless

Dutch player, made it a part of his mission to keep me down to protect his status as the star of the team. What's worse, the club's leadership saw his destructive behaviors but did nothing. They just hoped that the results would come in.

In the evenings, during my rides home to my parents (I was still living in my parents' home), I began to feel stressed about the dysfunctional dynamics of the team. But I didn't want to share my struggle with anybody. I felt the need to show a brave face, so as not to give space to many of my parents' worries. The last thing I wanted them to say was, "See, we always knew it. This is not a good path. This is not for you."

After struggling for some time to earn a spot in the starting eleven, I finally got the courage to bring it up to our head coach. It was hard for me, but I was respectful, and he recognized that I was putting in a lot of work. He reassured me and told me that I deserved more and that I would get more playing time soon. But shortly after, a new high-profile forward was signed, who captured the eyes of the coaches and fans, and pushed me further down the ranks. I waited for the coach to put me in the starting lineup like he promised. But he didn't keep his word. Needless to say, I was angry and frustrated, and I felt betrayed.

I once again asked the head coach for some time to discuss matters. This time, he said that he had never committed to giving me more playing time. And then he started to get loud. He was trying to shut me down. He said in no uncertain terms that I had no right to complain, that I should feel lucky to even be sitting on the bench. "Who do you think you are?" he shouted. He made me feel small. But later, in the locker room, he made me feel even smaller. He humiliated me in front of the entire team. "If you don't like it here, you can pack up and leave!" he yelled at me with the whole team watching. I was stunned. I couldn't believe that this was our leader, the person I was supposed to look up to and admire, shutting me down in the most ruthless way. It was a true loss of innocence for me. From then on, I started to see a very dark side of professional sports and how much one toxic leader can poison the atmosphere of a team. And yet, after that horrible interaction, the head coach put me on the field every match, like a strange reward for surviving his venom. But he also never spoke to me directly again, like an ongoing parallel punishment.

I couldn't handle it. Mentally and emotionally, I was at a low point, and it was a fight to show my personal best performance in such a high-stakes and pressure-filled environment. This frustrated me even more. When I didn't feel well, I didn't play well. The more I thought about it, I concluded: You have to work even harder and train more than the others to eventually be rewarded.

Consequently, I accepted that the club put me on loan with other clubs to allow for more playing time. And I added many extra training sessions to not only fight my way back but to make the next steps to achieve my long-game vision of playing for the Swiss National A-team. All of this led to massive overtraining, and eventually, my body gave out. Two ACL ruptures in my right knee in two years derailed my career. These weren't the result of tackles or fouls but from my unchecked intensity and my refusal to ease up. After nearly five years in professional football, my dream was slipping away. The pain wasn't just physical. There was pain in my soul, too. I had not yet reached my full potential. Out of all the games that I played professionally for FC Basel, I felt I had truly performed at my potential in only about twenty percent of the matches.

Looking back, now through the lens of a performance coach and psychologist, with decades of critical distance, I can make better sense of what at the time seemed like terrible luck, personal failure, and the inability to perform at the highest level. My story and the lessons that I learned became the foundation of my work helping top talents, first in sports and then in business, navigate high-pressure environments to achieve extraordinary results. I learned critical lessons through this experience.

First, about courage and risk-taking, I realized that at pivotal moments when you need to take a risk, it is so important to have the support from your inner circle. At that young age, my inner circle was mainly my parents, but they were unable to be in that fully supportive role due to their own fears, which they transmitted to me. I also learned how adversity can be isolating. In professional football, very rarely is there someone who guides you through the emotional and mental toll. As a result, I learned early that the mental game matters just as much as the physical, and that raw talent alone is not enough. That mental toughness and emotional resilience separate those who succeed from those who falter. And finally, that context is everything. The belief that true talent always rises to the top is just that, a myth. Environment, leadership, culture, teamwork, and emotional support play such an enormous role.

Let's now shift to business, and I'll share more about what that means in real-time practice.

PART I

WORLD-CLASS IS
NO COINCIDENCE

EVERYONE ON THE TEAM
PLAYS AN IMPORTANT ROLE:
But a Few Make All the Difference

We're no longer in the locker room now. We're instead in an office tower of a corporation. This likely describes your life day-to-day: You lead a team, a department, a division, a function, maybe even a whole company. There are no easy days at work as each day is a mental challenge, where you juggle important meetings, often back-to-back, then in between conversations with employees, requests from customers, and negotiate and interface with business partners, your management, or a steering committee or board of directors. While it is not a physical job, like a professional athlete, each day can feel like an obstacle course through the many competing priorities: Things you want to do in your role, things you need to do, things you should do, at times, firefighting and managing crises, often with little time for planning and creativity.

As a result, day after day feels like running a marathon with a never-ending series of sprints. It's very intense. But you know that you are not in this alone. You lead an organization and a team, and when it's all working well, they are all in sync with you and your vision. Together, you are like rowers in a racing boat, hopefully all moving together in a harmonious and powerful rhythm, pulling toward the same finish line. All the rowers have different strengths and areas of expertise, but they are all strong rowers.

Now, step back for a moment and review who is in the boat. If you could only row with a select few, who would you point to straight away? Who would you not want to lose? Who are the key rowers that you put in the boat time and time again, knowing that they will deliver? Who are the very few with world-class potential to take your company's game to the next level?

How Many Actually Do Make a Difference?

Major companies, just like professional sports teams, take care to recruit and promote from a very select talent pool, seeking individuals who have the right education, background, track record, competencies, experience, and personality to thrive and make an impact in challenging roles. They are carefully vetted before hiring or promoting, and once in the role, are expected to perform at a very high level. Within this context, many corporate teams are composed of a remarkable number of high performers. It's like a professional sports team, where everyone, whether on the field or the bench, has risen to the top ranks to be there.

Then there are the very select few within this high-performing organization who show a truly exceptional talent. They are the ones who have the potential to achieve extraordinary things, who push the whole team further, under the most pressing conditions. They are the ones who are not just satisfied with the status quo on a high level. They are going the furthest, taking the risks that pay off, delivering outstanding performance as a baseline, creating innovative solutions, and inspiring others to level up. It's these special talents that make you think: These are the Game Changers. If they quit, we've got a real problem!

Companies constantly debate at the highest level what they can do to drive innovation, to unleash the potential of their best people, and to surface the most revolutionary ideas. I have seen this phenomenon first-hand, having worked with hundreds of participants in key talent programs and coaching clients. Even among individuals classified as "overachievers," or individuals who regularly exceed their performance targets, this share of individuals with game-changer potential still remains quite small. Based on my observations and the data from my programs, the actual number of individuals with game-changer potential in an organization will most likely be in the low single-digit percentage, probably even in the per-mill range. Of course, depending on the industry, field, and company, these numbers may vary a little, but not very much.

This leads to two critical key questions. First, have you identified these individuals in your team, department, division, function, or company? Second, how much time have you invested in these "stars" of your organization today, last week, or the previous year? And how does that compare with the time and effort you spend on the rest of the team? Even those who are having performance issues? You know who I mean. In the world of business, we experience the same phenomenon again and again: While the most promising individuals with game-changer potential tend to reliably deliver excellent results, many executives tend to devote a large portion of their management time and energy to the lesser performers and "problem cases" of the business unit.

As a result, it is not uncommon for leaders to frame this challenge with a certain mindset: "As a leader, it's my role to support the team members who are not meeting expectations and help them improve. For the exceptional ones, I should step out of their way and leave them to get on with what they are doing." And it's probably a natural assumption that the most elite in your teams were selected for abilities to work independently, be a self-starter, to be highly self-motivated and dedicated, and therefore not require much of your leadership. Rather, the space and autonomy given can almost be considered a reward. But if you compare this to the top level of competitive sports, such an approach would simply be unheard of. Imagine an Olympic champion whose coach gave them the least time and focus, only so that they could help the lesser-ranked with modest potential climb a bit further.

If you want to achieve ambitious goals in sports, you invest in the best. Anything else would be absurd. Companies seeking the best minds invest large sums of money and time in recruitment and assessments. They develop plans that aim to secure the next generation of senior leaders. But once the high potentials are on board, often a strange process unfolds: The attention of leadership shifts. The more outstanding an employee, the less time is dedicated to them. Management spends its time focused on managing the weaker colleagues, leaving the strongest to fend for themselves. "They can get by on their own, they can manage," is a common refrain by managers. These game-changing employees are even gifted additional tasks with the knowledge that they will reliably complete them. Instead of giving them more space to work on game-changing ideas, they are given more everyday tasks that don't move the needle in the long term. To me, this is unwise as it threatens the success of your business in the long run.

Where Leadership Makes The Most Difference

Let there be no misunderstanding. I am not arguing that you should concentrate entirely on a very small group of top-performing individuals with the greatest potential. This is not a sustainable leadership strategy either, as it wouldn't give the well-deserved attention and recognition, nor would it do justice to the many solid and strong performers in your organization. Rather, I am arguing that it is critical to prevent the opposite extreme, where you let your concentration and focus be absorbed almost exclusively by the smaller groups of low performers. And when I say, "low performers," this is a relative statement. In a team of extremely talented individuals, lower performers may still be working at a relatively high level, but they pale in comparison to their elite peers.

Consider taking time to reflect on which assignments, activities, and leadership opportunities have the potential for the greatest impact on the overall results and positioning in the market. I call these "high-impact" activities because they are highly relevant for the current and future success of a department or company. These activities result in innovation, growth, and productivity.

Then think carefully about how to distribute and delegate high-impact activities wisely and intentionally. In most cases, only a few key people are suitable for these high-impact activities. These individuals have the intellect, the strategic and innovative mindset, the ability to withstand higher pressure, can bear the corresponding high level of responsibility, and deliver outstanding performance in changing and adverse business environments. But when you do so, remember that it will take your time and effort to offer them targeted high-quality support and specific leadership as they step into this greater responsibility. You should not simply pass on and burden them with ever more projects that don't move the needle. You must be at their side as a strong and supportive leader, making a deliberate choice to invest your time in clearing obstacles and actively lending them your support and guidance for breakthrough moments.

This is extremely important because leading in this way is key to creating or maintaining the momentum for success, as well as retaining the best individuals in the company. Think about it: When was the last time you sat down with the best people in your department and discussed together what further contribution they could make to the future success of the company? If the usual end-of-year performance reviews come to mind, this isn't what I mean. End-of-year discussions have often become a routine exercise of reviewing predetermined goals and performance indicators and setting the goals for the next year. Of course, this is very important. But what I mean, however, is scheduling regular, organized, focused, and substantial exchanges between you and your top performers with game-changer potential, in addition to the year-end reviews and goal-setting meetings.

In these regular exchanges, together you can deep dive and focus on the future, and where they could make a true difference on top of the enormous value that they already bring. When you share your experience, expertise, and insights with your most promising individuals, they see your commitment to their overall success and how you are invested in bringing out the best in them. They can see that you do this not out of a sense of duty, but out of your ongoing desire for their success and your genuine interest in them, and their role in the organization. In this way, you show them that you have a clear ambition to help them reach their full potential.

There is a certain magic when a leader and their top individuals with game-changer potential have this regular exchange about high-impact activities that will shape their success in the future, and not just about the task at hand and the performance targets. A Winning Match stands for the ideal combination between an ambitious individual with game-changer potential and their leader, acting as their guide, sparring partner, and coach, in regular, honest, challenging, and highly supportive interactions. When this match works, you will have the basis to create extraordinary results through your Game Changers.

A Winning Match thrives on moments of intense debate on a wide range of topics. Sometimes it is about specific and highly relevant business questions or problems, where leaders and employees make lasting progress at the factual level and deepen their trusting collaboration. Other times, it is more strategic or abstract and future-focused, moving outside of the day-to-day operations to exploring a creative concept, a new way of doing things, challenging a norm, or thinking entirely differently based on an outside inspiration or insight. Only with these kinds of regular points of exchange will you find the chance to go beyond the daily topics into something bigger. Such Winning Match moments combine an ambitious, sometimes even ruthless, substantial debate with the highest level of mutual respect and openness. They are challenging and productive discussions. They are moments of connection that you both can eagerly await and that create a sustained dialogue with massive value over time.

As a fundamental for creating breakthrough decisions through Winning Match moments, you, as the leader, need to be intentional and strategic with how you plan for these to take place. One thing I realized very early in my work as an executive coach is that, when I go through the daily routines with senior executives and business leaders, they are often shocked to discover how little time they have for regular, performance-breakthrough discussions with their key employees on future topics. This is because they are very often tied up with all the other important tasks. Some of them barely manage to adequately prepare for these critical meetings. They share a feeling of running behind and squeezing in their one-on-ones on top of the daily priorities, not quite giving it the time and preparation that it deserves.

On the other hand, the individuals with game-changer

potential clearly express a strong desire for planned, regular, direct sparring with their leaders, to get to the heart of things and to make progress on what really moves the needle now and in the future. But what they often get in reality, however, is the standard performance talk twice a year, and their one-on-one meetings are entirely focused on day-to-day projects and deliverables. Over time, they get disappointed. They don't see a way to connect with their leaders in a way where they feel appreciated and valued for what makes them different and the additional value they can bring.

Interestingly, many companies have installed certain processes for the systematic handling of employees who fall short of their expected performance. Those include the notorious Performance or People Improvement Plans, or PIPs, that are used by many companies. In essence, the PIP is a structured measure to try and help so-called underperformers meet their set targets, or to chart out officially their inability to comply. A PIP is typically triggered after an unsatisfactory performance assessment in the end-of-year review, when the leader formally checks boxes such as "targets not achieved or only partially achieved." From the manager's perspective, this is never a great outcome. At the end of the year, after exhausting months of hard work for the manager, with feedback and efforts to compensate for the lack of their performance, they will kick off the new year by taking on the creation of an employee's performance improvement plan, with additional one-on-one meetings to track progress. It feels like an additional burden, and certainly, has legal aspects that need to be considered. But despite all these efforts, it doesn't always result in turning things around.

Imagine if the same efforts were invested in the Game Changers in your organization. What if each year, you co-created and designed high-performance plans for these individuals with world-class potential? And then you scheduled one-on-ones that were focused on closely supporting their idea creation and implementation. What could all this accomplish? Remarkably much! More on the why, when, and how in the chapters to come. But first, back to what is often a common reality.

As already mentioned, companies invest in a closer personal support for the low performers, while those top performers identified as high potentials are often sent to standardized leadership programs. These programs are important for continuous learning and development, and provide the opportunity to build a new network. While these programs will help individuals further grow, they are very often not specific enough. Let me put it clearly: You shouldn't ever think of outsourcing Winning Match moments. It must be a priority of your personal leadership agenda. Those who are truly outstanding have to be specifically challenged and encouraged by their leaders to create maximum value for the organization, in the present and the future. Many companies, however, have not yet established systematic approaches and processes that enable individuals with game-changer potential to be continuously focused on and strategically supported by their leadership.

The fallout from this can be disastrous. Individuals with game-changer potential who are not able to fully thrive in the position where they are, and with the leadership they get, will most likely begin to explore where they could find a better situation, usually a competitor company. Another, yet low possibility, is that the employee scales down their engagement out of frustration or resignation. Maybe they stick with the company or role because they see other reasons to stay, like a nice location or benefits. So, they decide to lower their expectations and do just enough good work, no longer the extra effort. In parallel, they wait for a good moment and offer to move on.

All of these outcomes mean that you will never get the full value from your best people, and you risk losing your people with the highest potential. I therefore recommend: Start immediately with targeted support for your best. Make one of your priorities to make your best people even better. It is one of the best investments you can make, with a high chance that it will result in a huge return.

WHAT SETS
GAME CHANGERS APART?

Individuals with game-changer potential are highly ambitious, extremely talented, strategic, extraordinarily disciplined, and focused. As I said before, they don't just stand out from the crowd. They have the potential to eclipse the crowd entirely. But let's get specific. What do I identify as the key components of people with game-changer potential who can produce exceptional performance, continuously and sustainably, at the highest level? I have identified four essential characteristics that define individuals with game-changer potential:

- Passion
- Desire for Feedback
- Ability to Transform Input into Action
- Mental Toughness

While some of these traits may seem familiar, their depth and real-world application are often misunderstood.

Passion is more than just enthusiasm; desire for feedback is more than being confident in the face of criticism; transforming input into action is more than the ability to initiate change; and mental toughness is more than keeping composure under pressure. Let's go deeper into these characteristics so that you can understand what they can really mean and why I consider these to be so critical for the people with game-changer potential in any industry, field, or organization.

PASSION: When Game Changers Are in Their Element

Passion is a real corporate buzzword these days, and one that I feel gets quite overused. Scroll just a few minutes on LinkedIn and see how many people talk about their passion for their work, their team, their last business trip, their newest product, and their latest campaign. Passion in this context becomes synonymous with excitement for something, such as a task, a role, or a cause.

But individuals with game-changer potential experience passion as something beyond just excitement. Their passion shows up as a deep, intrinsic commitment to mastering challenges and achieving excellence. What fuels them is not just a superficial or passing interest, but rather activities and pursuits that are multifaceted, challenging, and difficult to master. This type of passion generates the focused energy required to solve complex problems, execute ideas with precision, and push through adversity. It creates an unshakable internal contract with one's goals, a determination that is not easily swayed by obstacles or temporary setbacks.

A useful analogy is mountaineering. Many people admire mountains, enjoy their beauty, and appreciate hiking and winter sports where they experience the mountains up close. But compare that with elite mountain climbers and alpinists who are driven by an all-consuming passion, constantly pushing their limits, planning new expeditions, and embracing failure as part of the journey. Their passion is not just about appreciation; rather, it is about the challenge, the relentless pursuit, and eventual mastery. They burn with an intense desire to plan the next expedition that nobody has ever done. As a result, their satisfaction and joy with reaching the summit are fleeting. Soon, they are thinking about the next summit to reach. If they are not able to reach their goal, they recommit to the next attempt, seeking to overcome what stood in the way of their success. This is a critical differentiator. Many say that they have a passion for something, but then give up when the going gets tough or when they don't see quick results. Or when they get bored or find something else that's new and exciting. That's most people.

Game Changers persist even when results are not immediate. They refine their skills continuously, viewing setbacks as part of their journey rather than as signs to quit. They continuously provide outstanding performances and are deeply convinced that they are in their element. They see every step, including every misstep, as part of their journey to achieving big goals. They strive to perfect their skills and to develop new ones as they approach their passions with persistence. They know that they are in it for the long haul and that it's not just a fleeting interest.

They can also face the real possibility of total failure. Those who strive for high goals run a much higher risk of failing in front of others, which can lead to embarrassment in the eyes of the public and feelings of shame. Compare that to someone who remains in the comparatively safe realm of mediocrity and doesn't take that risk. Game Changers are not satisfied with playing it safe. They want to push the boundaries, and not just from time to time. Those who do something with real passion suffer doubly if they remain below their potential. Failure gnaws at them. What is crucial, however, is that this suffering does not lead to resignation, but instead fuels them to try again, and allows them to continuously transform to reach the goal. They don't recommit to just working harder. They know they need to work differently.

Passion, however, exists on a continuum. On the most positive side, passion becomes playful. This is when the activity or role is perceived as truly fulfilling. Game Changers feel fully absorbed and in their element when performing their activities. They find it deeply satisfying to work in this way. When passion is playful, you feel in the flow and have an enormous capacity for singular focus. The most effective performers are keeping their passion focused and playful most of the time, and mobilizing a necessary amount of obsessive passion and willpower as fuel to keep going for periods to work through roadblocks or setbacks. They set an extremely high bar for themselves and have a deep desire to achieve big goals, inspiring themselves and others to be a part of it. While they are often successful because of their creativity and tenacity, when they do not achieve their goals, you can feel their suffering. But not in a way where they are defeated, resigned, or blaming themselves, others, or the environment. The failure sparks a moment of reflection with a renewed commitment to transform, work differently and find a new approach for a better outcome.

DESIRE FOR FEEDBACK: Game Changers Want to Hear the Truth

Feedback from friends, family, and colleagues is not always nice. It can hurt. It can shine a light on some of our deepest insecurities or fears. Feedback can surface things that we don't like in ourselves, things we have struggled to master, and places where we are weak or unsure. As a result, it requires a strong competence to accept feedback, to take it in, and to process it earnestly and productively. Many claim to be open to feedback, but when faced with it, they instinctively defend themselves or explain away their mistakes. Some go on the offensive to protect their ego instead of seriously considering what was said and exploring it from that other person's perspective.

But individuals with game-changer potential take a different approach. They ask the following questions: Can you tell me what I am doing wrong in this situation? Can you tell me why you think that course of action did not go well? They actively seek inputs, even when they can be difficult to hear. Overall, they do not shy away from unpleasant situations because they know how to regulate their reactions and emotions. As a result, they can accept feedback without being drawn into conflict or defensiveness. All in all, what makes Game Changers stand out is that they approach feedback as a tool for growth rather than as an attack on their competence, character, or personality.

A defining trait of Game Changers is their desire to surround themselves with people who challenge them. Rather than avoiding tough conversations, they welcome them, knowing that their ability to continuously learn and adapt is necessary for their long-term success. That said, not all feedback is useful. In addition to the desire for feedback and input, Game Changers have also developed the ability to differentiate between valuable insights and unhelpful noise. They recognize the importance of listening to those with deep expertise and honorable intentions while ignoring feedback that lacks substance or is driven by an ulterior motive. This ability to filter and prioritize feedback is crucial. They do not blindly accept all input but instead critically assess it, filtering out what is most meaningful, relevant, and actionable. Then, they take the steps to adapt, keeping themselves accountable for consequent actions and their individual growth. With the decision to adapt, they take 100 percent responsibility for the change that they choose to make. Individuals with game-changer potential know that their personal development is very much based on and accelerated by critical, direct, honest, and constructive feedback and input.

When I coach individuals with game-changer potential, I often observe a certain impatience already in the first of our interactions. They want something to change, to improve, and they are more than ready to do what it takes for that to happen. Game Changers cultivate a mindset where adaptation is not an exception but a norm, viewing themselves as never finished or fully developed, but as flexible and dynamic. No matter where they stand, there is always still something they can learn, adapt, and improve, and they welcome new qualitative inputs. Game Changers are convinced of their ability to develop and don't focus on what they can't do, but rather on what they can't do yet. They want to hear the truth about why something doesn't work as they expect. They look for new inputs so they can adapt. They see change as an opportunity rather than a threat, and are grateful for honest input. And with that, they create the foundation for game-changing success.

ABILITY TO TRANSFORM INPUT INTO ACTION: Game Changers Are Masters of Implementation

Recognizing the need for change is one thing; taking the hard or uncomfortable steps to implement change effectively is another. Once feedback has been shared and input is processed, many people understand objectively what they need to do, but then struggle to take action. As humans, we have an affinity for security, familiarity, the status quo, and the safety of our comfort zones where we can operate with our predictable patterns. We avoid discomfort and are ashamed of our fear of not being able to master new challenges.

Theoretically, most of us know that change is necessary to improve for the better. It's while implementing change that something practical is applied. It takes place in the doing and requires commitment, dedication, and a flexible mindset. Game Changers know this. That's why they excel at translating feedback and new information into decisive action and can move beyond mere readiness for change into forward movement and a plan to succeed. That's because if new input makes sense to Game Changers, they implement it immediately after one conversation. Why? For one, they recognize that standing still is not an option in competitive environments.

There is hardly any domain where the ability to transform input into action is as vital as in competitive sports. Performance limits are constantly moving, new competitors arise all the time, and physical and mental strength have to be redefined over and over again. Elite athletes must constantly refine their technique, adjust their strategy based on competition, and work with coaches to push their physical and mental limits. It is hard to get to the top. And it is hard to stay at the top. Transforming new insights and inputs into action is key to both getting to and staying at the top.

The same principle applies in the corporate world. Performance thresholds in business continue to increase as today's competitive landscape becomes ever more fierce, cutthroat, and fast-paced thanks to new and disruptive technologies and increasing customer demands and expectations. Game Changers in this arena continuously adapt, refine their approach, and integrate new insights into their decision-making process. They constantly process feedback, new insights, research, data, and emerging trends and rapidly integrate them into strategies. They don't try to hold on for as long as possible using the old methods with the hopes that they will somehow work. They instead develop an instinct for making changes as early as possible, long before alarm bells are ringing, and when there is no other choice. Game Changers quickly pivot as needed, and can take on new information and fluctuating contexts quickly and decisively. Their ability to implement new inputs with speed and precision is a hallmark of their success.

MENTAL TOUGHNESS: Game Changers Know How to Meet the Moment

The ability to perform under massive pressure is the fourth defining trait of Game Changers. All of us have career-defining moments where the stakes are incredibly high, and when we have to show up and perform at our very best. Mental toughness ensures that these moments are met with confidence and clarity, instead of doubt, anxiety, or paralysis.

In the world of sports, the best trainers and coaches will tell you that excellent physical conditioning and mastery of the technical aspects of a sport are essential for a champion. At the very top, however, this is the minimum requirement to be competitive. It is not only physical fitness or technical brilliance that turn very good players into absolute champions, but rather their ability to give their top performances even under extreme conditions and to demonstrate their best game, under pressure, every time they show up for competition.

Moments like these are what competitors train for, and not just in the gym or practice. World-class athletes have learned to attain a clear mind though things like visualizing the moment, finding their flow, and managing their nervous system to turn down the volume of their anxious thoughts, negative self-talk, and physical sensations of discomfort. This allows them to completely be in the moment, fully engaged in the here and now, so they can focus on what matters the most. Together, this is what gives game-changing athletes the confidence and determination to make the right next move and to perform at their full potential under enormous pressure.

I observe this not only in elite sports but in all domains. Game Changers have realized that they can only reach their full potential if they build up their mental toughness so that they can show up and be at their best when it matters the most. As a result, Game Changers are the ones who don't spin out in their emotions during pivotal moments. They can acknowledge what is at stake and, at times, feel stress and nervousness, but thanks to their ability to self-regulate their minds, they can also effectively regulate their emotions. At the same time, Game Changers have developed high-impact strategies to productively manage their mental, emotional, and physical energy, especially during crunch time.

———

The bottom line is this: Individuals with game-changer potential can be extraordinary contributors to the success of your organization. Their defining traits of passion, desire for feedback, ability to put inputs into action, and mental toughness set them apart to make big things happen. That's why leaders and managers need to recognize these qualities in their people. Once identified, plan to give these individuals opportunities that challenge them, push their limits, and allow them to grow and use their potential to make a real difference. When supported effectively, Game Changers don't just succeed; they can transform the organizations around them.

In summary, the four characteristics of individuals with game-changer potential are identifiable. Pay close attention to the following signs that you have a Game Changer in your midst:

First, the passion of Game Changers shows up as a deep, intrinsic commitment to mastering challenges and achieving excellence. They persist even when results are hard to attain, and their passion helps them push through to success. Setbacks are seen as moments to continue exploring and adapting—as part of their journey, not as a sign to give up.

Second, Game Changers know that the road to the extraordinary is very much based on high-quality inputs and accelerated by critical, direct, honest, and constructive feedback. They seek it out, accept it gracefully and without defensiveness, and evaluate it constructively.

Third, Game Changers excel at translating feedback and new information into decisive action, moving beyond just a readiness for change into forward movement and actions to succeed. They don't waste time overthinking.

Finally, Game Changers can manage their focus and emotions in times of enormous pressure and adversity. They have developed effective strategies to manage their mental, emotional, and physical energy in the face of the most challenging situations.

Figure 1 shows the four characteristics of Game Changers at a glance, and the following overview highlights some of the key behavioral indicators of each characteristic of Game Changers.

WINNING MATCH

Game Changer

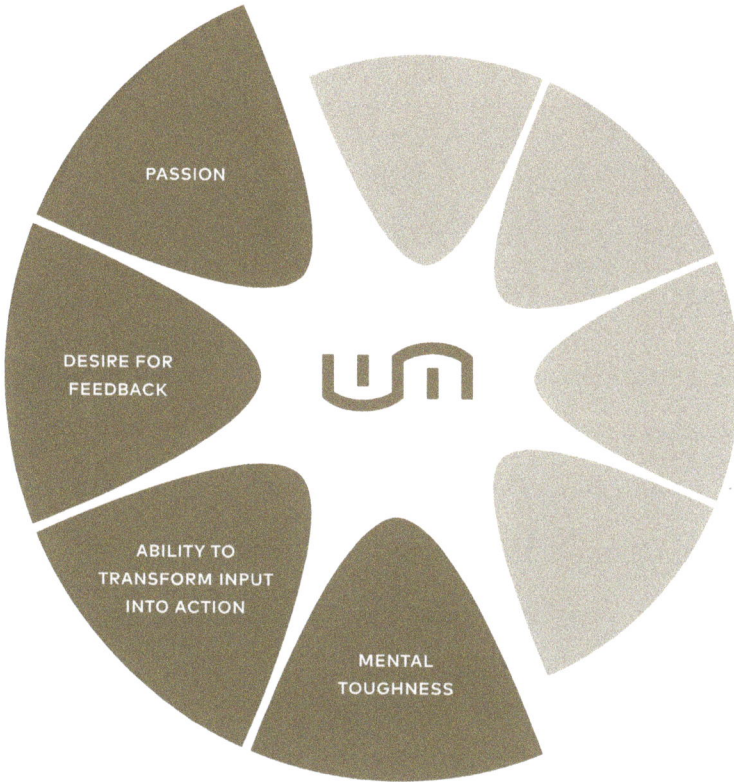

Fig. 1: Characteristics of Game Changers at a glance.

HOW TO RECOGNIZE INDIVIDUALS WITH GAME-CHANGER POTENTIAL

PASSION

1. Game Changers identify 100 percent with their undertaking and feel a personal connection to what they do. Whenever their playful passion has reached its limit, they push through by activating some obsessive passion and willpower.

2. Game Changers are fueled by a powerful internal desire to create impact. Their passion is rooted in a personal sense of purpose. They aren't just working to succeed, the are driven to change something for the better, whether it is a product, a system, a team, or a broader cause.

3. Game Changers thrive on challenge and exploration. They feel a deep sense of frustration and personally suffer when they do not fulfill their potential. Their passion shows up as a hunger to learn, improve, and push boundaries. This keeps them moving forward, even when others would settle.

HOW TO RECOGNIZE INDIVIDUALS WITH GAME-CHANGER POTENTIAL

DESIRE FOR FEEDBACK

1. Game Changers actively look for new high-quality inputs and demand open and direct feedback from the people whom they value, even when it can be tough to hear. That's because they know that this information is essential for ultimate success and their growth.

2. Game Changers evaluate the feedback they receive without defensiveness. Critical words do not damage their self-esteem. They listen to learn, rather than listen to defend.

3. Game Changers carefully evaluate who to listen to and who to ignore. They understand that not all input and feedback is delivered with substance or the right intentions. Game Changers can differentiate between feedback given honestly and feedback with ulterior motives.

HOW TO RECOGNIZE INDIVIDUALS WITH GAME-CHANGER POTENTIAL

ABILITY TO TRANSFORM INPUT INTO ACTION

1. Game Changers fundamentally look at change as an opportunity to achieve even more. The need to change is not seen as a threat. They understand themselves as constantly evolving and view themselves as dynamic and capable of change.

2. Game Changers act proactively and with prudence. They prepare for and initiate changes before the circumstances force them to do so. That is why they can quickly pivot instead of defaulting to old ways.

3. When a new input or piece of information makes sense to them, Game Changers implement it immediately and decisively. They don't need to hear the same critical information several times before they begin to act on it.

MENTAL TOUGHNESS

1. In crunch time, Game Changers respond with strength and resilience and consistently show up at their best in key performance moments. They do this by concentrating on the execution of what is essential and by controlling their focus, nerves, and emotions.

2. Game Changers stick to their good habits to manage their energy so that they can continue to perform at their best in high-intensity environments. They know that maintaining mental, emotional, and physical energy is key to lasting success.

3. To sustain high performance, Game Changers consciously design their private lives to allow regular disconnection, rest and recharge. Supportive relationships, especially with family and friends, offer grounding and perspective beyond their competitive roles.

Now that we took a deep dive into what character-izes a Game Changer, and how to identify them, these are the resulting questions: How can you help the Game Changers you have identified unlock their true potential? What is going to make the difference for them? The next part of my story and Part II of this book will provide you with answers.

MY STORY CONTINUES

I already painted a picture of what football meant to me when I was young. Football was my life. I had an enormous, playful, at times also obsessive, passion for the sport and reaching its highest level. I certainly had a great desire for input on how to take my talent and build my skills to the highest standard of excellence. I sought out feedback and ways to improve from coaches, even though, toward the end of my time playing, I found fewer people I could trust to help me develop. As ready as I was to put those inputs into action to further develop my game, in the end, it was without strong and supportive leadership. And in that incredibly intense environment on the pro team, I lacked the mental toughness and emotional resilience to sustain my success, particularly in the toxic culture and the dysfunctional team I was in.

So, my next severe knee injury was an inflection point. In 1995, at the age of twenty-two, I was in the hospital with my second ACL injury. I knew the road to recovery would be brutal because my doctors told me so. While they promised to do whatever they could to help me play at the highest level again, they were also realistic. My knee wasn't healing well, and my coordination might never fully return.

Then reality hit me: I had gone from being one of the biggest football talents in Switzerland to the one who never quite made it. At least, I had a pre-university education and some savings to fall back on, though it wasn't enough money to retire early. My biggest fear, however, wasn't just about the money. It was whether I would ever find something that ignited the same passion and intensity that football had given me.

For the next few years, I existed with intense inner turmoil. I lived with grueling rehabilitation, painful self-reflection, and a search for purpose. I was thankfully still under contract and was covered by insurance, so despite being injured, I was still being paid a salary and had a financial safety net. But what was next? Due to my rather unique life journey thus far, I had always felt that I didn't belong 100 percent to one specific environment or place. On one hand, I was an elite athlete, and I had fully committed myself to that life and that sense of purpose. On the other hand, a few months after the last of a series of surgeries, I was starting to feel like an ex-athlete, exiting a very rare and privileged world. Outside of my life as an athlete, I always had a high level of intellectual curiosity. I also connected well with people, navigating easily between different groups.

During my rehabilitation, as my connection to the football club and my athlete peers started to change, I realized the discomfort of living between worlds, having not found a group or a context that I fully identified with. I still had friends from outside of football circles, but many had moved forward in their studies while I was stuck navigating an uncertain future. I finally had to accept the painful reality that my window for a return to professional football had closed. And I had no clear idea where to go next.

Looking back, I realized that during the most challenging moments of my career, I had no one to open up and talk to, no one to spar with, no one to mentor me, and help be a trusted guide through the mental strain of elite sports. It was very Darwinistic: You are either strong enough to make it through on your own, or you're not. If you drop out, there's a line of others desperate to take your spot. Vulnerability and self-reflection were seen as weaknesses. Therefore, almost nobody talked about their worries and fears. Such conversations were associated with being not strong enough to make it. This led to a certain form of isolation, as the last thing I wanted to convey was that I was not strong enough.

In the early and mid-1990s in Switzerland, the world of sports and performance psychology was in its complete infancy. Mental coaching for athletes was practically nonexistent, and there were only a few models and established frameworks available, and most of them were very theoretical. It was during this time, after my career as a professional football player had ended, that I started to think more about the isolation that I felt and the tough culture that I had endured. I felt that I missed the key tools to face the adversity and challenges to get to the top. And if I felt this way, how many other players in that locker room experienced those same feelings? Surely others in similar situations felt the same. But nobody dared to talk about their needs because they didn't want to be seen as weak. I began to wonder if, with all of my experiences, I could become the person they could talk to and turn to for help and support. Could I become the person I had needed during my playing days?

I also knew that if I was going to help others, I needed more than just my own experiences. I needed real expertise, to not only be the person who understands but who could actually help. So, using all my savings, I enrolled in psychology courses at the University of Basel. The first two years were difficult; the theoretical nature of the psychology field felt disconnected from my journey as an elite athlete. Research methods, statistics, and the classical psychology curriculum engaged me intellectually, but I wasn't sure how to apply them in a way that aligned with my experiences in professional sport.

To make matters more complicated, because I was still under contract, I had certain obligations besides my studies. I was juggling rehab and club obligations, along with my university coursework. One of my psychology professors, Dr. Gerhard Steiner, a former fellow at Stanford University in the United States, was a highly disciplined, rigorous academic. His philosophy was clear: presence in class was mandatory and was the only way to pass the course. I was struggling with my other daytime commitments, which ate into my availability for class, but I was determined to make it work. I approached Professor Steiner, who was at the time the dean and a well-respected person of authority, and explained my situation in a personal conversation. There were hundreds of students, and I wasn't sure if he would even take me seriously, maybe even having some bias against athletes or anyone who couldn't be present 100 percent of the time in his class. But his response surprised me. He appreciated that I took the effort to meet him personally. He also thanked me for my honesty and told me: If you can't make it to the lectures, then you've got to read extensively.

So, that's what I did. I read as much of the research and literature as I could find, in addition to the required course texts. Two years later, his assistant reached out to me and said that Professor Steiner wanted to meet me in his office, the same one I had met him in two years prior. This time, he wanted to see me after grading my exam. "I didn't expect this," he said. Professor Steiner was surprised that I had kept to my commitment, that I went above and beyond the assigned reading, and that I ended up earning the highest score despite missing lectures. He said to me, "I am impressed. So, what do you want to do with this knowledge, and where do you see your future?"

That conversation changed everything. I told him that I found academic psychology too theoretical and disconnected from the reality of elite performance and sports. I told him my story and how I wanted to apply what I was learning to help athletes gain the mental strength and emotional resilience they needed to sustain the highest performance. Professor Steiner responded with an offer: If I could find a university that combined psychology with practical sports and performance applications, he would count it toward my degree. That led me to explore international research. During my reading marathon, I discovered two professors, Dr. John Salmela and Dr. Terry Orlick, who were both prominent leaders in applied sports psychology. I wrote them each a letter, shared my story, and asked each of them if I could visit and attend some of their lectures. They wrote back and were happy to welcome me as a visiting student at the University of Ottawa in Canada. I took what was left of my savings and invested in this opportunity to study abroad.

The experience was transformative. Unlike what felt like a rigid European approach, the methods in North America were dynamic, practical, and tailored to real-world performance. Having found like-minded academics with a lot of autonomy, I immersed myself in everything I could learn about mental strength techniques, visualization, emotional regulation, and high-performance psychology. Inspired and focused, I developed my first mental training program, specifically designed for injured athletes. That's when *Comeback* was born, my structured approach for incorporating capabilities like positive self-talk, healing visualization, and pain management techniques. It was the program I wished had existed when I was recovering from injury. I knew that it had the potential to make a huge difference for elite athletes, especially for those who are at a very vulnerable point in their career, when they have to recover from a severe injury.

In parallel, to test my acquired methods, I offered my services to the university's women's soccer team. They embraced the program and my services, and the results spoke for themselves. The Ottawa Gee-Gees won the national championship against the odds, crediting their mental training program as a key factor. That moment of validation, of seeing my work impact a team's success, confirmed that I was on the path I was meant to be on. I had found my new purpose. It was such a time of clarity for me, knowing that I could have an impact in the field of elite sports.

Upon my return to Basel, I was ready to share my work with my peers and professors and take my research further. I reached out to the Rennbahnklinik, a renowned private sports clinic where international top athletes go for surgery and rehabilitation. I was lucky to get a few minutes on the phone with the head surgeon and co-founder, Dr. Bernhard Segesser, a visionary in his field. Despite being overworked, he took the time to listen to my story and immediately saw the potential. But he was honest: "I don't have time for this, but I love it. And I know it's important. I can't pay you, but I'll give you full access to our athletes, staff, and resources."

With Dr. Segesser's support, I began tracking the psychological impact of injuries among the patients at the clinic and ran studies based on my research on how mental training influenced healing. I designed a unique longitudinal study, measuring recovery rates, setbacks, and resilience strategies over extended periods. I started to see many of the hypotheses confirmed in my research. I proposed turning this research into a PhD, and my clinic sponsor helped me secure funding. There were some bureaucratic hurdles, since this wasn't an established doctoral path in Switzerland. But despite that, with the support of Dr. Guido Schilling, I secured sponsorship through ETH Zurich, widely regarded as one of the top institutions for science and technology worldwide, and the University of Zurich, ensuring my research had the highest academic credibility.

Not even three years later, I earned my PhD in Applied Psychology. I was now the only person in my family history with a PhD and—as a bonus fun fact—I am the only player in more than 130 years of FC Basel history to have earned a PhD. My research at the time was one of the most comprehensive studies on mental resilience in injury recovery. That academic milestone should have been the highlight of my transition from pro football player to Doctor of Psychology. A likely next step would have been to teach in this burgeoning field at a Swiss University, especially as I had already delivered my first guest lectures at the ETH Zurich. But what happened next changed everything.

I was about to complete my PhD. Since I was still known in the local sports world as having been one of the most promising talents, the media covered my path to becoming a performance psychologist in regular articles. One of these articles landed in the hands of Peter Carter, the then-coach of rising junior tennis star Roger Federer. Roger was a promising talent from the Basel area. At the time, he was world ranked ten as a junior. Peter reached out and invited me to work with Roger. I had to be honest. I told Peter in our first conversation that I had no deep expertise whatsoever about the game of tennis. But he emphasized that they weren't looking for a tennis expert but someone who deeply understood the demands of high-performance sport and has the ability to create mental focus and emotional regulation. Well, this was my place. I felt immediately welcomed.

For the next two years, I was part of Roger's team, witnessing his evolution firsthand. I sat with his family, strategized with him on his mental approach, and worked with him to navigate the emotional highs and lows of professional tennis. Within the first six months, Roger climbed from ranking ten to ranking one junior in the world. He then went on to play on the ATP tour. I still remember when we prepared for his first professional match in Gstaad. Soon after, Roger made his debut with a wild card at the ATP 500 tournament in Basel, the city where we both came from. Roger lost against American superstar André Agassi in the first round, but he was playing a great match. A year later, Roger made it to the quarter-finals to almost beat Britain's Tim Henman, who was ranked world No. 7 at the time.

Soon after, Novartis, one of the world's top pharmaceutical companies, headquartered in Basel, approached me through the University of Basel, inviting me to run leadership training workshops. That marked my entry into the corporate world. I was invited to share my insights on high performance and how it can be implemented in corporations. I loved it. I realized that the two worlds are not very far apart. Corporate leaders recognized the value of my work early on, and demand for it grew rapidly. It was an experience that reaffirmed my belief in the power of performance psychology and leadership coaching, not just in sports but in all high-performance environments, especially business.

Moving forward, I didn't want to abandon sports entirely, nor did I want to disappear into the world of big corporate consulting firms. Instead, I carved out a space where I could bridge the two, applying high-performance psychology to elite athletes and business leadership. I decided to do it exactly the way I felt it had to be—my way, at the intersection of elite psychology, executive leadership, and world-class performance. Which meant that it was time to start my coaching practice as an entrepreneur.

Of course, launching a start-up company as a solo entrepreneur in a field that was not widely known or accepted was a clear risk. It was the unconventional path that, at the time, almost nobody had taken. This time, however, I was ready to follow my instincts. I remembered the conflict I felt when I had to decide which club I should join as a professional player. But instead of giving in to fear, I told myself now was not the time for compromise. I knew that I had everything in me to go all in. I felt deeply that there was a need for what I could offer. It gave me a strong sense of purpose.

My wife, Sabrina, has always been my greatest source of encouragement. We met during my final year of university and started to date. From the very beginning, she saw something in the vision I had for my future. I still remember her words: "Chris, go for it. I know you'll be great. If the business doesn't generate a profit right away, I'll cover our expenses. We'll figure it out together."

She didn't just embolden me. Sabrina gave me her full confidence and backing. Thus, her unwavering support further strengthened my determination to pursue something uncertain, something bold. At the time, we were both well aware of the odds—nearly 60 percent of all startups fail within the first three years. But instead of letting that deter us, we made a pact: If the business became profitable within that time frame, I'd continue. If not, I'd explore a more traditional path, maybe in academia or at a company.

I was mentally and emotionally ready to take the risk, and I was fully supported by the closest person to me. This foundation helped me approach the new and unknown with excitement, positivity, determination, courage, and clarity. It turned out to be the right bet. By the fourth month, it was already a self-sustaining business. And over the years, it led to new heights and spheres that I never imagined. Who knew that I would ever fulfill my dream and realize my vision of winning something as big as the World Cup, but in a different role than I had originally imagined? And not as the protagonist but as a partner behind the scenes? I have been privileged to work with extraordinary executives, leaders, board members, and entrepreneurs who achieved exceptional success. And with outstanding athletes who became (multiple times) Olympic Champions, World Champions, and Champions League Winners. What an amazing ride it's been.

While my playing career didn't unfold the way I had hoped, it gave me meaningful lessons that proved invaluable later on. Yes, I had many disappointments from that time, but it was that exact journey that led me to something even more meaningful in the end. Over time, life came full circle. In 1999, right before Sabrina started her first corporate job and just as I was to start my PhD, we decided to take some time off. We had both recently completed our master's degrees, and we were living lean as I used up almost all the money for university. I decided to spend the last of my football funds on a few weeks of travel, including a US road trip passing through Las Vegas. As a little splurge, we got tickets to the legendary Cirque du Soleil show "O". I had never seen anything like it. It was amazing, spectacular, and fascinating. Twenty-five years later, I was working with Cirque du Soleil's executive team for a number of years to support their successful rebound after the pandemic. One of our sessions was in the iconic Bellagio in Las Vegas. I brought Sabrina—and our two sons Leonardo and Tiziano—to spend the weekend. We also saw "O" again. Exactly twenty-five years later, after the restart of my journey. This time, we were in the best seats, thanks to a personal invitation. It was very emotional for me and Sabrina, remembering that time of uncertainty and reinvention, where I was not clear where the road ahead would take me.

What initially began from a place of loss ultimately became a journey of discovery and purpose. The lessons I learned from football, injury, and reinvention have shaped me into the person and coach I am today. If I can take away one key lesson from my transformation from player to performance psychologist and executive coach, it is that the role of great leadership cannot be underestimated. I had a strong passion for the field of performance psychology, but I would have never achieved what I did had I done it alone. Along the way, I had mentors, teachers, and leaders who saw my potential, nurtured my curiosity and drive, pushed me, believed in me, and helped open doors and clear obstacles in my path. Several key individuals took a risk with me and allowed me to enter new territories because they saw how I wanted to change the game. Great leaders have the power to help others push the boundaries. I was blessed to experience this firsthand. Through this, I found purpose and peace in dedicating my life to the service of others, making my knowledge and experience available to support others to sustainably perform at their full potential, take smart risks, push their boundaries, fulfill their aspirations, build cohesive organizations, lead others with inspiration, and reach their dreams.

PART II

TOP PERFORMANCE REQUIRES TOP LEADERSHIP

THE BEST DO NOT PREVAIL NO MATTER WHAT:
Game Changers Need Leadership Champions!

Let's start with a decisive insight, one that I have seen proven time and time again in my coaching. It is a false belief to say, "Great talents prevail anyway." And having faith in that false belief can stand in the way of your excellence as a leader.

Let me explain. Just think about highly gifted students. It is not uncommon that some of the most gifted students don't excel in school. In fact, some even fail their courses and drop out. The difficulty for gifted students is that when the environment doesn't match their intellect or talent, they can get bored. Having so much mental energy with no outlet, many either rebel and misbehave or simply shut down. In those cases, specialized and competent teachers are needed who can first recognize those talented students, even if their grades are not showing it, and then help them stretch and grow their talent in a targeted and skillful manner.

Something similar can happen in companies. Top individuals with the potential for the extraordinary may stagnate in positions and with tasks that do not match their performance potential. In many cases, they are not given the opportunity to stretch and show what they are capable of. Many potential Game Changers are instead given tasks or projects where they can make some incremental improvements, or, worst case, ones that get locked up in internal bureaucracy. They are also assigned the tasks and projects necessary for smooth operations, but not the high-impact activities that make a real difference to the longer-term growth of the company. For passionate Game Changers who are ready and willing to make a difference, leading to a deep sense of frustration.

All in all, for Game Changers to deliver outstanding performances that match their potential, they need a trusted partner. They need you to be their Leadership Champion. As I have said before, when a Game Changer is paired with a Leadership Champion, the collaboration will very likely yield extraordinary results, benefiting not just the team but the entire company. A Winning Match is this ideal win-win situation because it brings individuals together who can collaborate in ideal ways to essentially match. This is how you can make the best even better.

We know that Game Changers can be decisive and persistent. However, when they recognize that their environment does not permit them to contribute their full potential, they will sooner or later become impatient and feel unfulfilled. Disillusioned Game Changers will eventually seek a different position with different leadership that matches their vision, passion, and talent so they can unleash their full potential. From a company perspective, this is devastating. To see Game Changers leaving is very disruptive, and it is a visible example of missed opportunities and untapped potential.

So, which qualities do Leadership Champions need to match with a Game Changer? As mentioned, Leadership Champions need to first be excellent scouts for Game Changers and for individuals with game-changer potential. Once you have identified these individuals, serving as a trusted sparring partner becomes essential. I will discuss the concept of sparring in more detail in the next chapters.

Next, there are two additional crucial characteristics of Leadership Champions. They include the ambition for the overarching success and generosity. Let's first talk about ambition, and how Leadership Champions embody ambition beyond their personal achievements, but for the shared of the team, the company, and for their customers and stakeholders, and everyone they serve.

THE AMBITION
FOR OVERARCHING SUCCESS

Ambitious leaders want to win and to build, not just something important but lasting. They don't just want to preserve the status quo. Motivated leaders want to make a significant difference as they are not satisfied with being good enough. Rather, they strive for greatness, impact, and legacy.

The drivers for an individual's ambition are varied. Some are driven by external motivation, such as money, material gains, fame, titles, and public recognition. While others have internal motivations: The satisfaction of delivering top performance in line with their highest standards, gaining knowledge and new insights, and knowing that their hard work paid off and made a real difference for others.

But one's personal ambition, if taken too far, can also have a negative side and may be destructive to overall success. This side of ambition can be characterized by egocentricity, short-sightedness, lack of empathy, ruthlessness, recklessness, and indifference. This type of ambition can encourage leaders to use people for their own gains and exploit their company's power and influence for personal advantage. This is the antithesis of being a Leadership Champion.

For Leadership Champions, ambition has a different direction. Leadership Champions seize their leadership tasks with determination and commit themselves completely to the achievement of their company's purpose and overarching goals. They make full use of their leadership potential and keep their individual goals as secondary to the organization's goals. That's because Leadership Champions have a stronger desire for the overarching success of the company and for creating maximum value for its customers and stakeholders, more than for their own personal success. Their ambition, their desire to win, is not primarily ego-driven, but collectively aimed. The primary motivation of Leadership Champions is to lead the company, the division, the team, and individuals to maximum performance. As a result, their highest impetus is creating all the conditions and interactions necessary for the optimal achievement of goals, for the company as a whole, and especially also for Game Changers.

True Leadership Champions act as a supporting force who seek to bring together the company's aspirations and goals with the talents in the organization in the best possible way. This is of paramount importance because a Winning Match can only exist when participants do not outdo each other with their individual interests but aim to achieve together what is best for the whole—the customer, the company, and anyone positively impacted by their success.

Now, do you have what it takes to become an essential part of a Winning Match? First, to become a Leadership Champion, you must build and possess a strong and evolved ambition to lead others and then yourself to success. That's because, as a Leadership Champion, you must always keep your eye on the overarching collective goals first. And because Game Changers have developed the highest level of passion for excellence, they seek out leaders who share a strong, collectively-oriented ambition. In this way, Game Changers and Leadership Champions match in their motivation level: A maximum level of passion for the extraordinary connects with a maximum level of ambition for impact and the overarching success. It is in this way that both the Game Changers and the Leadership Champions care for and want to drive the greatest possible overall outcomes.

That's why, for you as a Leadership Champion, it is of key importance that your ambition to lead to success, to progress your leadership potential, and to constantly improve, is compatible with the overall purpose and success of your Game Changers. Therefore, it is crucial to distinguish between two types of ambition: Collectively-oriented ambition for overarching success and me-oriented pursuit of personal gains. Leadership-relevant decisions ideally integrate personal targets with the overarching goals of the company. What is good for the whole should, in principle, also be good for you as an individual. In situations where this is not possible, Leadership Champions prioritize collectively-oriented ambition. This means you are always primarily concerned with the overarching success of the company rather than gaining personal advantages.

Consistently putting the importance of your own goals behind the overarching success of the company sends far-reaching positive signals across the organization. The message you send is: "What we are doing here and what we strive for together is more important than what I could personally benefit from."

So, how do you, as the Leadership Champion, express your collectively-oriented ambition in real time? Here are some aspects to consider:

- Provide clarity about the overarching targets of the organization, the purpose and strategy of the company, and how your team's area connects and contributes to the larger whole.

- Develop a good understanding of what it will take for the overall success and have an inspiring way of communicating a compelling vision and strategy, as well as targets and performance indicators with your teams.

- Offer support so that others can also contribute maximally to the whole's overall success, and inspire others with your motivation to contribute to the collective outcome.

- Constantly seek optimization potential for overall success in your areas of direct influence, and in other areas of the organization as well.

- Confront immediately any lack of commitment by others that could jeopardize all-around success in a solution-oriented and productive manner.

- Ensure the optimal positioning of your team members' roles and functions toward the collective, overarching success.

- Set high-performance standards for individuals throughout the organization as a whole.

- Bring in the best possible experts and related competencies to the team when it is relevant to achieving overall success.

- Be a role model for cross-functional collaboration. Offer to hand over resources and employees to other divisions and departments of the company when they are urgently needed to achieve an overarching goal. Place your personal goals behind others for overall success.

- Protect your teams and employees from other departments, individuals, and stakeholders that don't act in the best interests of the company or who are transparently pursuing their own interests and targets by actively driving alignment.

- Step back and, if necessary, relinquish resources for the betterment of the company. This might include supporting changes that increase sustainable overall success, but eliminate or make one's role redundant.

All in all, you can see how much the ambition of Leadership Champions is clearly oriented toward the bigger picture and the overall success of the company. This means for you as a leader, to become and be a true Leadership Champion, you must personally go through a transition whereby you value and prioritize collective success more than personal success.

Let's look at such a transition with one of my business clients.

Mark

Mark was an ambitious leader who prided himself on leaving nothing to chance. With his high-level scientific education, his strong intellect, and his drive, he could be relied upon to always deliver first-class results. As a scientific mind with a research background, he had encyclopedic knowledge that set him apart. He always wanted to understand everything in detail, as if taking a microscope to all aspects of his work. But as his role changed and he took on more senior positions with greater leadership responsibility, this detail orientation, or occasionally obsession, was beginning to stand in the way of his success. With each upward move, being close to the details became increasingly difficult. And once he became the research and development (R&D) head of a global pharmaceutical company, where he was next in line, it would be completely impossible.

In our executive coaching, we zeroed in on the cost of his detail orientation. Once considered one of his superpowers, it was now holding him back.

Mark's microscopic interest in all aspects of various projects, programs, and processes was his essence. He loved the research, he loved the science, and he had a genuine passion for his work and felt a high level of commitment to excellence. Never leaving something untried, no stone unturned, was natural for Mark. And he was applauded with awards, promotions, and increased responsibility to lead others in return.

Now, as the leader of a much larger team of experts, Mark continued to rely on his default way of working. But this caused friction in the organization. Some of his leading talents found his constant monitoring and deep inquisitiveness to be bordering on micromanagement. Mark himself often felt stressed, as there were no longer enough hours in the day to keep tabs on all of the individuals in his team and all aspects of their projects. As a result, Mark would work late at night and on weekends, so he rarely started the week feeling refreshed.

When I interviewed individuals on his team about Mark, they would say:

"Mark knows so much, but he doesn't trust us. He is always tinkering with our work and asking us to explain our methods."

When I asked Mark, he would say: "Relentlessly overseeing all aspects of the work and being on top of everything is my duty as the leader of the team."

At the heart of it, Mark saw himself as the most senior expert, tasked with running a team of specialists. He didn't view himself as a Leadership Champion who embraces full responsibility for his stewardship and the overarching success of the company. This was uncomfortable for him because it meant that instead of concerning himself with countless details, Mark would now have to focus more and more on his leadership capabilities and what he could do to unlock the greatest potential in his organization. In all, Mark had to shift from being the one knowing it all to paving the way for others to excel.

My focus was clear: Work with Mark to help him rethink his leadership, his motivation, and his detail orientation. Mark needed to embrace the idea that his ambition must be primarily collectively-oriented and redefined to answer the question: What will successful leadership look like for me? A shift toward collective success would mean trusting his people to deliver excellence, while his role would be to create the environment where the best people can step up and deliver the extraordinary.

Mark and I started to look at the costs of his desire to be completely up to date in all areas, to always be familiar with the newest trends and scientific data, and to be known as one of the best experts in his field. All of these interests were taking away from his role as a Leadership Champion.

Although Mark would never entirely abandon reading scientific journals and all the latest literature, during our coaching, we looked for ways to put that in perspective with learning about how to lead others to success. We didn't want to limit his strong ambition and desire to win, but broaden it beyond science to leadership as a domain. It was in this way that we started to shift Mark's thinking about his success. Where he once measured his success by ranking his performance and that of some of his teams, we started to focus on the effect that his leadership has on others and their contribution to the overall success of the company. It was important for me that Mark could learn to build up both types of his ambition to a high extent. And get it in the right order of priority.

Some months later, after intensive coaching work, Mark started to fully embrace his role as a Leadership Champion. His team noticed a remarkable difference and shift in his leadership behavior. They felt that he had more trust in their work, they were more empowered, and felt equally inspired and supported. Thereafter, Mark gained a reputation as being not just an amazing scientific expert but an excellent motivational leader who was deeply committed to the company's purpose and success. And the kind of leader that can bring out the best in others.

Today, Mark is a successful head of R&D at a pharmaceutical corporation and one of the most respected and appreciated leaders in the company and the entire industry. In his previous position, Mark clearly used his ambition for overarching success by moving significant resources from his own department to another that was in urgent need of support for a mission-critical program. This convinced the CEO of Mark's foresight. In Mark, he observed a Leadership Champion and a partner who saw the overarching success as his highest priority. Mark's example illustrates how the best must develop from one level to the next to be a Leadership Champion, and how such a transition adds huge value to a company.

This transition is far from easy. I have seen this also in other competitive environments. For example, in the world of elite sports, I have noticed many top contenders who, after highly successful careers as athletes, decided to pursue a career as a head coach. They see it as a natural next step, and most of them expect that the transition from athlete to coach will be seamless. But after so many years focused on their individual goals and achievements, performing at their absolute highest limit, winning championships, medals, world records, even being voted Most Valuable Player, when it is time to shift their ambition toward a truly collective success, where making others better and the overall achievements of a team are what matters most, they struggle to pivot. That's because deep inside, they still want to be the stars who capture the limelight. Very often, this leads to poor leadership performance, often causing personality clashes with the best on the team, because they cannot truly connect with others on a motivational level.

It is no wonder, then, that the next key component of a Leadership Champion is generosity. It is this quality that causes them to leave a lasting, positive impact on others. It is also another critical component for creating a Winning Match.

GENEROSITY AND THE DESIRE TO MAKE A DIFFERENCE IN OTHERS

Like any competitive environment, the corporate environment can be ruthless. There is a common belief that to get ahead and to achieve a lot in a business career, it is every person for themself. But Leadership Champions know better and defy the norm. One of the key factors that sets them apart is their generosity combined with their desire to make a difference in others. These central components form the foundation of all of their beliefs and actions as leaders.

Many leaders I speak to tend to believe that they are generous. However, I can see a distinct difference between most leaders and Leadership Champions. For one, most leaders apply what I call "conditional generosity." They provide their people with time, resources, knowledge, and access to important networks. But in return, they think of their own benefit. When leaders apply conditional generosity, there is always an expectation of receiving something in return.

True Leadership Champions, however, act and lead from a different place. They apply maximum generosity, based on a great deal of unselfishness, altruism, and trust. This means that their high investment of time, intellect, emotions, efforts, and potentially even financial resources for others goes without the expectation of a certain result or a direct return on investment. This is what I call "unconditional generosity," the type that is needed for a Winning Match.

For you as a Leadership Champion, it means making your own network available unconditionally, and especially helping your people with game-changer potential form strong alliances and unlock possibilities to collaborate. It also means passing on your know-how in your area of expertise, as well as your understanding of the organizational context, to help others navigate complexity and to help them succeed. This willingness to unconditionally share is critical. And it only truly works without expecting a direct return on investment, not viewing the world as a quid pro quo. You understand that generous actions don't always yield concrete results, that being generous as a regular practice will at times lead to unexpected benefits in ways you cannot always predict. Rather, your knowledge, expertise, and your acquired contacts are considered free goods that should be used by all. Because the goal is clearly to achieve the extraordinary with and through others, and with that, make others great.

But how exactly does this happen? The generosity of Leadership Champions is expressed through their support for Game Changers in empowering them as quickly as possible to deal with challenges independently and according to their own judgment. In the long run, the role of the Leadership Champion is not to be the rescue squad, tasked with eliminating acute problems as soon as possible. That's because it is far more important to help the Game Changers find and develop their own unique strategies to solve critical problems on their own and to empower them for independence.

Now don't forget, Game Changers have the desire to constantly develop themselves. They therefore wish for feedback and input, so that they can contribute as much as possible to the overall success of the company. If your Game Changers experience you as a Leadership Champion who shows up with a high degree of generosity, they will reliably benefit from your knowledge, your wisdom, and your valuable contacts. They can rely on you, knowing that you won't attach conditions or demand some kind of payment in return. It is when your generosity matches with the Game Changer's desire for feedback and ability to put input into action that you match decisively at the attitude level with your Game Changers.

Here are a couple of action steps that you can do to lead with unconditional generosity:

- Proactively offer your time, access to your network, your wisdom and experience, your creative ideas, and organizational know-how as free goods to your Game Changers.

- Develop the necessary level of self-esteem and self-confidence as a leader to realize that, with your support, your Game Changers may someday be even better than yourself. Feel deep satisfaction when you have contributed so positively and actively to their development toward excellence.

- Transfer responsibility for important, highly visible tasks to your Game Changers, even if, as a top executive, you might lose some accolades and visibility. Commit to making your Game Changer look successful.

- Relieve your Game Changers by taking over parts of their standard tasks so that they can concentrate sufficiently on their new challenges.

- Support and provide constructive feedback after your Game Changer makes an important mistake or bungles a big task. Then, articulate expectations for how they can better behave in similar situations in the future.

- Help your Game Changer prepare before an important key performance moment, meeting or presentation. Provide plenty of positive reinforcement whenever they make a positive impact.

- Back up your Game Changer if they suffer unjustified negative behavior from others.

- Show perseverance, patience, and resilience in developing your Game Changers, and expect no return on investment for your generosity.

Now, let's consider a real-life example that illustrates the transformative power of Leadership Champions' generosity and desire to make a difference in others.

Martha

Martha had taken over as the leader of a division and was now reporting to the CEO. She had a solid start in the role. During her first couple of months, she scouted Kelly, a team member with game-changer potential. In addition to Kelly's high degree of passion, desire for feedback and input, ability to transform input into action, and her mental toughness, Kelly was highly intelligent, had an extraordinarily good eye for details, and at the same time was able to keep the bigger picture. Martha had a high level of confidence in Kelly's subject matter expertise and her innovative approach to the work. She was constantly impressed by Kelly's ability to put forward unique and innovative ideas that challenged the status quo and could really make a difference for the business.

However, a key aspect of Kelly's role was to build coalitions internally and advocate for transformative changes and new and innovative ideas. But whenever Kelly presented to the executive team, she fell well below her true potential. In a one-on-one setting,

Kelly could dazzle others with her knowledge of the topic and her excitement for the transformative potential of a new idea or process. Her enthusiasm was infectious, and she brought the idea to life.

But in front of the executive team, a panel, or a steering committee, it was a totally different story. You could see Kelly's lack of presentation skills. She had a hard time staying on message, repeated herself, and forgot important points. Kelly's meandering would confuse her audience. It was clear that they didn't get it, and soon lost their patience. "Kelly's way of presenting is a complete disaster. We don't really get what she wants to say," was the direct feedback from the CEO. He started to question Martha and why she had put so much confidence in Kelly.

In her new role, Martha simply couldn't afford continued negative criticism and perception of this kind. She felt that her judgment was in question and that Kelly's poor performance in front of the executive team was casting a shadow on her and her team. But Martha believed in Kelly's ideas and felt that they had the potential to make a big difference.

She was frustrated that the ideas were getting lost due to Kelly's poor presentation skills and lack of clarity. "What should I do now?" Martha asked me in coaching.

I replied with a question. I asked her to think about how she was approaching the situation. She told me that she felt that none of her peers, nor the CEO, were able to see Kelly's true talent and potential. That the packed executive board room was not the place where Kelly was able to shine. Martha wondered if she would have to take over and do the presentations herself, even though Kelly was far more knowledge-able about the topic.

I challenged her with the following questions: "Do you think this is a sustainable solution? Do you think taking over the presentations and being the spokes-person for these game-changing ideas will fix the issue in the long term? Do you really want to help Kelly make a change?"

"Of course!" Martha replied promptly.

"So, how does taking over the next presentation help in the end? You can do it for her once or twice, to salvage the situation and protect Kelly from losing credibility in the short term. But then, how does it help you? And how does it help Kelly?" I asked again.

Martha thought for a short while and said, "You are right. If I take over now, this fixes the problem in the short term. This is very important now. But doing it on a longer basis would not help Kelly in her development. It would also reinforce the assumptions of those who doubt her and believe that Kelly isn't up to the task."

I then threw another possibility into the discussion: "Is prepping Kelly before every presentation an option for you?"

Martha thought about it briefly and replied, "Yes, and no. I am not sure that this would solve the problem in a lasting way. I know the tactics that I use to persuade while presenting, but Kelly needs to learn this in her own authentic way. I am happy to share with her all the things that I do at the executive team level, but I am not sure that I am the best coach for this."

I asked her to consider a third option: "How about then giving Kelly the opportunity to be coached professionally on her presenting by a communications expert who specializes in helping people who struggle in front of such a senior audience like the executive team?"

Martha's reaction came quickly, "I know that this might be a costly investment, but if we could get Kelly a really good coach, I am sure she would make big strides in just a few weeks. This would give Kelly the greatest chance to develop where it truly matters for her."

I could see in that moment that Martha really cared about Kelly and was committed to her success and professional development. From her point of view, she could see Kelly falling below her potential in front of a very senior audience, but she believed that she could master this important skill with the right support.

Martha then said, "I will organize this special coaching because I feel strongly that someone as talented as Kelly should be able to shine in front of any audience. Her ideas are too important to get overlooked, and she could really help with the company's growth."

Martha acted as a true Leadership Champion with the desire to make a lasting impact on others for the betterment of Kelly and the company. In several 1:1s with Kelly, Martha shared what she was leaning on when presenting in front of the executive team and the board. Furthermore, Martha's proposal for targeted, professional coaching was well-received by Kelly, who, over time, was able to improve her presentation and communication skills in front of any audience.

Martha was later thrilled when a colleague on the leadership team took her aside and said, "I was really impressed by Kelly's latest presentation. I finally felt like I got what she had been trying to tell us. I am considering funding a small-scale pilot so that we can test drive this new idea. I think it has a ton of potential."

Bringing your unconditional generosity and your desire to positively spark a change in others in a lasting way is critical to make the best even better. Let us now dig deep into this practice and see how you can act as a valued sparring partner to your Game Changers.

SPARRING: Leadership Capabilities for Champions

How much leadership do Game Changers need? This is probably the wrong question, because people with game-changer potential do not need less or more, but above all, a different, very special type of leadership interaction.

Traditionally, leadership is practiced in many corporations in the form of regular appointments and meetings, and in more formal ways through target setting and assessment. The employees report on their progress to their manager on a weekly or monthly basis as part of a standing meeting cadence. In these meetings, the leader and employee check in and discuss where things stand, any blockers, and what the next weeks will bring. More detailed strategic discussions take place quarterly, or once or twice a year. In these meetings, the goals of an employee are agreed upon, and the achievements of previous goals are checked. This is a tried-and-true method, and it is usually only adapted when problems or issues arise.

However, there is now a broad consensus across management and leadership literature that work should, in principle, be done collaboratively, meaning that employees should be heard and be involved in decision-making. In addition, all team members should be equally heard and considered, and everyone's unique personality and style should be respected.

Of course, all of these approaches have their positives, but I am convinced that they cannot fully do justice to the extraordinary potential of Game Changers. That's because for Game Changers, you need to go beyond a classical management approach. For Game Changers, sparring is the most effective path to success.

I think of sparring as it is used in sports like boxing, where athletes train by fighting seriously with each other, but according to rules and with equipment that prevents injuries as much as possible. Likewise, in business, sparring is harder and more confrontational than traditional conversations. But it is also more flexible and open-ended, as it is oriented toward the goals and ambitions of the Game Changer and puts them to the test. While traditional management techniques aim to maximize the performance of all employees, modern sparring opens up the possibility to develop and use the full performance potential of those who can play in another league.

Sparring is a targeted, success-oriented form of intervention that addresses both immediate and long-term challenges. The contents of a sparring session are often future-oriented, where sparring partners together further develop innovative ideas to drive growth and productivity. It can be highly strategic, where you look at different angles to drive lasting change or transformation. A sparring session can also just as well be quite practical or tactical. For example, when you work together through scenarios in preparation for a critical negotiation. Sparring is useful to stress test or interrogate important decisions, especially when there is incomplete information or significant ambiguity. Sparring can also be valuable as a kind of retrospective by taking an objective and close look at root causes in the case of failure.

As a result, sparring is not always planned with a lengthy lead-up but sometimes is scheduled at short notice. It is important for you as the leading sparring partner to go along with the pace of your Game Changers, taking a clear position yourself, and therefore offering a clear source of counterbalance. Unlike in traditional coaching, the objective of sparring is not to primarily support the other person in finding their solution to fix a situation, but to also have an open, and if necessary, controversial debate to create long-term impact. As the sparring partner, therefore, your wealth of experience and expertise are required, as well as your commitment to be personally involved in co-creating the decisions that lead toward extraordinary outcomes.

Sparring partners put themselves exclusively at the service of the other. It is not about one's victory or success, but about a targeted interaction to bring the Game Changer forward so that they can achieve the extraordinary in the real world. Therefore, to me, sparring is one of the most critical and comprehensive leadership competencies that leaders need to acquire. Sparring involves a certain number of concrete skills that are reflected on real levels by concrete behavior. In the following sections, I will introduce you to the key sparring principles and skills that I personally apply in my work and that I have witnessed Leadership Champions apply with their Game Changers.

FIVE MUST-HAVE SPARRING PRINCIPLES FOR LEADERSHIP CHAMPIONS

Let me introduce you to five sparring principles that, according to my experience, pave the way to extraordinary performances for Game Changers:

1. RESPECTFUL: Options instead of instructions
2. FLEXIBLE: Inspiration for growth instead of pressure to adjust
3. DEMANDING: Productive discomfort instead of harmony
4. MAXIMALLY SUPPORTIVE: Clearing the path instead of delivering fixes
5. PLAYFUL: Light-footed instead of heavy-handed

For each of these sparring principles to have an impact, you need specific sparring expertise and proficiency. Let's take a closer look at each of them.

#1 RESPECTFUL:
Options Instead of Instructions

Of course, every person deserves respect. By this, I mean appreciation of the person, their human dignity, and their right to be uniquely themselves. As a leader, you create an environment where trust and respect are at the core of your culture, and where differences co-exist. When interacting with your people, there is no place for personal attacks, rhetorical tricks, or any form of threats or manipulations whatsoever.

Sparring with Game Changers requires an additional form of respect: the Leadership Champion's appreciation of their counterpart's extraordinary potential and their ability to choose between different options. This means that when you spar with your Game Changer, you, as a Leadership Champion, do not argue from a position of hierarchy. Generally, you also do not give instructions.

When you enter into a sparring session with a Game Changer, you accept them as equal partners in the discussion. Rather, Leadership Champions and Game Changers work together, without any hierarchical boundaries, to find and co-create the best possible solution.

When sparring, the decision on how to proceed remains fundamentally with the Game Changer. You create an atmosphere of positive exchange, where you speak your mind openly, can honestly express concerns, and also point out any potential areas of weakness. That's because as a Leadership Champion, you put yourself in service of your Game Changers by affording them a trusted place where they can test and explore their own ideas, especially unconventional ones, without risk of ridicule. They, in turn, know that you will respectfully listen, contribute, and protect them from making big failures. And when there is a decision point, you ensure that the Game Changers are in the driver's seat.

Fig. 2: The sparring principle RESPECTFUL.

Equal footing, confrontation, and commitment are a powerful triad that defines respectful sparring. We will now look more closely at each of these three skills.

Equal Footing

What do I mean when I say that the hierarchy is suspended during a sparring session? As a Leadership Champion, a key fundamental is that you accept the Game Changers as your equal, and vice versa. You make yourself available as a partner for discussion so that the Game Changer can put their own ideas to a robust test and make them even better. The decision as to what they will do at the end is and must remain with them. During your first sparring session with a Game Changer, it is important to set this ground rule and to reinforce that your exchanges may be challenging, but they will always be respectful and at eye level. This can be enormously motivating.

For many successful managers and executives, sparring is not something that comes naturally. Absorbed by their tasks and confronted with little time and few resources, sometimes the hierarchical model of exchange is more comfortable as it requires little extra effort or self-reflection. But with Game Changers, there is a tremendous imperative to embrace the sparring approach. When you listen carefully and interact at eye level, in a respectful exchange, that is when you have the best chances that their ideas and innovative approaches will reveal themselves.

There are different ways that you can listen, and they have important differences:

LISTEN TO ASSERT

This kind of listening is about gaining your understanding of the problem in a relatively short period of time, and then waiting for a suitable moment in the course of the interaction where you can take over rhetorically. Your goal is not primarily to fully understand the broad motivations and perspectives of your Game Changers, but rather to be able to present your view on the matter. Often, managers leave such conversations with a good feeling that they have taught something. That is how convinced they are of their own opinions and expertise. But in doing so, they missed out on an opportunity for a Winning Match moment. Always remember: Sparring with Game Changers is about fully grasping a challenge or problem from their point of view, and then examining their proposed solutions together to see their potential for success. This does not happen if you are centered on imposing your own opinion, perspectives, or worldview.

LISTEN TO FIX

Your counterpart confronts you with new information, ideas, and input. Although you do listen attentively to your

Game Changers, mentally, you are already leaping ahead into solution mode, formulating what you have to do to solve the problems of others, or at least to actively contribute to the solution. The motivation is at the heart, positive, namely, the desire to lead your Game Changers to a state where they no longer experience the problem or challenge. But a pitfall of listen-to-fix mode is that you offer solutions to Game Changers' problems without supporting them to devise their own creative solutions. Listening to fix comes from a good intention, but is rarely fully appreciated by Game Changers. By doing this, you undermine their ability, innovation, and creativity to deal with challenges themselves.

LISTEN TO LEARN AND GUIDE

You listen carefully to your Game Changers to understand where exactly the challenge lies and what it means for them. Only when you, as a Leadership Champion, have completely grasped this will you be in a position to collaborate with your counterpart in helping them articulate their own solutions, and then putting them to the test. Make sure to regularly paraphrase and play back what you think you have heard from your Game Changers. Only when they have confirmed your understanding should you go one step further. To ensure this, ask your Game Changers to think aloud about the possible outcomes, positive and negative, of their proposed solutions. Point out any weaknesses or flaws respectfully, then talk your Game Changers through the potential consequences of each option, and ask what kind of support they might need to implement their ideas. The aim of listen to learn and guide is to go deeper into the issues and to completely understand your Game Changer's unique perspective, given the fact that you want to fully hand over the freedom to act. By listening to learn and guide, you show that you are willing to interact at eye level. Equal footing is the first of the sparring skills for a reason: It is the most important! If you can waive your formal hierarchical superiority, the chances of a productive Winning Match moment are much higher.

Confrontation

Confrontation is essential in the context of sparring. Sparring thrives on confrontation and healthy tension. Whether it is in the boxing ring or a corporate environment, the sparring partner seriously challenges their counterparts to help them get stronger. They do this by not making it easy for them. Sparring differs from real competition primarily in its objective. The sparring partner does not want to win or rise victorious over their opponent's weak points. Rather, they want to allow the other to see their weaker areas and improve on them, and at the same time, take their strong areas to an even better level. This means that you should voice uncomfortable truths, discuss worst-case scenarios, and examine counterarguments seriously and bluntly with your Game Changer. In such an interaction, both sides will benefit, especially Game Changers who are hungry for feedback and appreciate clarity and honesty.

For many Leadership Champions, it is not always easy to confront or to give a reality check. But you can introduce those tough observations by saying, "I would be a bad leader if I didn't tell you the following..." Such an introduction emphasizes that you, as a Leadership Champion, take your role seriously, even when it means spelling out unpleasant things unwaveringly.

At the same time, confrontation is always situational as it refers to an actual context. It contains definite facts, verbalizes personal emotions, and expresses clear expectations for the future. "I would be a bad leader if I didn't tell you the following..." also makes voicing critical words more bearable because you automatically remain more objective. Using this opening can give you the legitimacy to do the right thing and touch on a specific and difficult point precisely because, by failing to do so, you would be denying your Game Changer an opportunity to improve and grow.

Commitment

The most emotionally demanding component of sparring is supporting the decisions of the Game Changers in situations when you might have decided differently. If you have a varied opinion on how they should go about a specific challenge, it would be easy to think and say: "Well, I'm not convinced, but give it a try and see what happens" since at the end of the day, it's their problem and they will suffer the consequences if it fails. "At least, I told them that I would do it differently." Instead of doing this, I strongly invite you to use a different approach—a disagree and commit formula, that I've seen used in various companies. It is a concept where you can share that you might approach it differently, but are ready to debate their ideas to help them stress test and refine for the best outcome, and provide full support after extensive debate. Game Changers know that the debate will help their actions be better and more well-thought-through. And this reinforces that you are supportive and fully committed to their growth.

This support and commitment are highly encouraging. As we all know, a lack of support can be crippling. If a Game Changer's suggestion is answered with a lukewarm, "Okay, if you want..." or "Go ahead, but if it goes wrong, it's on you," then you can most probably expect the implementation to be riddled with some doubt and hesitation. And with that, an increased risk of failure becomes predetermined. "Disagree and commit" means plainly, "I would do it differently, but we don't have to have the same approaches. I am with you, I understand and respect your point of view. And I can see the potential that it will lead to success. I commit and I will be emotionally bought in, continue to be with you to help you succeed, and I will back you up if things go wrong."

In sparring with Game Changers, every question on the table will not have only one absolute correct answer. That's because there is much more to debate and decide on various options. In these scenarios, I refer to so-called problems as "unanswerable questions," as you must find a position concerning all the possible options, and their potential for a positive or negative impact on the outcome.

1. **Agree and commit:** This is where you intellectually agree with the approach suggested by the Game Changers. You like the idea and give assurance of your commitment and support during implementation.

2. **Neutral and commit:** You may feel neutral to the approach suggested by the Game Changers. But you carefully listened to their arguments, you feel that this can lead to success, and you have assured them of your commitment and support during implementation.

3. **Disagree and commit:** You actually may intellectually disagree with the approach suggested by the Game Changers. But you understand why they want to make the decision, feel that your points have been discussed with the right level of depth, and you can see a chance that the path forward can lead to success. Therefore, you fully buy in and you offer assurance of necessary support during implementation.

4. **Disagree and don't commit:** You intellectually disagree with the approach suggested by the Game Changers. At the same time, you deny them your support during implementation for very good reasons.

As a Leadership Champion, you only deny an employee your commitment if your concerns are extremely high. In concrete terms, you should only act this way if you fear that the Game Changers could jeopardize the overarching success of the business, because certain relevant points have not been sufficiently taken into account in their thought process. In these cases, you will enter into a transparent and open disagreement—disagree and don't commit— to address the exceptional situation as such. Concretely, this is an ideal moment to postpone the decision for the Game Changer and to take a step back. This may be the time to seek out more information and ideas, and then come back in a second sparring session where disagree and commit might be possible. With some distance and thought, new information and data, further options for action may also arise.

It is your responsibility as a Leadership Champion to ask yourself such critical questions: Am I against it because there are serious, objective reasons? Or am I against it because if the new proposal turns out to be a success, my judgment might be questioned? Is it also possible that my strategy could be exposed as second best? If you answer yes to the last two questions, then let it go! Because this means that there are no serious, objective reasons to oppose what your Game Changers are proposing.

It is much more your own ego that is preventing you from committing. Therefore, you should challenge yourself to give space for unconventional ideas, be open to learning from them, and be courageous in truly understanding your reactions and their motivations.

Here is an example of how respectful sparring between a Game Changer and her Leadership Champion, based on equal footing and confrontation, led to a strong and committed response.

Nathalie

I had been working with Nathalie, a senior executive, for a couple of years. Nathalie was reporting to the Global Head of Development (GHOD). She told me about one of her business units that had been recently moved to another country to reduce costs. The move made sense from that perspective; however, the performance and the results remained below expectations.

In one of their meetings, the GHOD asked Nathalie, "Do you think you have what it takes to turn this unit around?"

Nathalie had clear ideas for driving positive change. She observed that the current scope of work of different people in the country was not optimally distributed. Her boss, however, was unconvinced. She had the strong belief that the team members in the country were not capable enough, and that Nathalie should replace a large number of the team with new, more capable hires. She confronted Nathalie with her point of view that this could not be solved with the existing people in the unit, and that she felt that Nathalie had so much on her plate that it would be too much for her to manage.

Nathalie, on the other hand, was convinced that if she organized and assigned parts of the work differently, there would be a very good chance that this would lead to a successful implementation by the existing team members. She was also convinced that with some extra support for a short period of time, she would be able to lead the organization through this.

The GHOD was skeptical. She confronted Nathalie with her concerns and worries that Nathalie would run too thin and, as a consequence, not be able to succeed with this business unit. She also had very real concerns that while Nathalie was focused on this turnaround in the other country, she could lose her impact with her other important mandates at head-quarters. They ended the discussion with the GHOD saying in essence: "I disagree and don't commit."

Nathalie needed this sparring session to think more deeply. She took the effort to speak to all the key team members of the specific business unit again and drafted a new setup with the existing team, immediately making some initial changes in the allocation of tasks and workload. Nathalie started to see some positive signals, but then realized quickly that she would not be fully able to manage this from a distance; she had to be on-site from time to time to provide the necessary leadership and guidance to make it successful in the mid- and long-term.

Therefore, she engaged with her boss in another sparring session. Nathalie aimed to make it clear to her that she had made some adjustments and that her first interventions were starting to pay off. Nathalie could report early progress, but if the business unit needed to be transformed, it could not be successfully done by her working exclusively from headquarters. It required her presence on-site.

The GHOD recognized that Nathalie had made some significant efforts to achieve progress already. She could see her commitment and that she was thinking beyond the original proposal. She was now listening to understand and willing to change her original opinion. Ultimately, she engaged with Nathalie at eye level and on equal footing.

Nathalie immediately observed the positive shift in the discussion. The GHOD challenged her, but also acknowledged where she had proven her wrong. After listening attentively to Nathalie, her boss said,

"If anyone can do that, it's you. Let's talk about how you can delegate some of your tasks here at headquarters so you can be even more focused on this turnaround. And if being on-site is critical, then let's make it happen. What else do you need to be successful?"

Nathalie was empowered to hire some experienced team members on a temporary basis at headquarters and abroad, and she could be where she was needed to be at the time. The willingness of her boss to give her this commitment was necessary for Nathalie, and quickly, she showed positive results. Nathalie managed to maintain her strong performance in headquarters and, at the same time, to intervene successfully and with lasting impact in the business unit abroad.

The results were fantastic. Not only was Nathalie seen as a leader who brought the existing teams together more efficiently and functionally, but the executive team was very pleased that the turnaround of the business unit was done in the most cost-efficient manner.

#2 FLEXIBLE:
Inspiration for Growth Instead
of Pressure to Adjust

The larger companies are, the more complex they can become. This is why processes, guiding principles, committees, and standardized requirements are put in place to regulate their ways of working. This cannot be completely avoided. Even the most agile and flexible companies still have a certain level of structures and processes to help them align and achieve common goals. But we know that Game Changers can be disruptive and challenge the status quo. So, how do Game Changers fit into this picture?

Especially for those with game-changer potential, companies and leaders must be flexible, particularly in designing the development opportunities to help them shape their careers. Game Changers usually have a clear vision of their future, so only offering them generic or standard paths may leave them uninspired and risk forcing a square peg into a round hole.

This isn't meant to devalue the standard career and development plans. However, they usually rely on conforming to a set model and the specific needs of Game Changers can be easily overlooked.

In addition, as many companies strive for efficiency and profitability, it is not unlikely to have too few employees rather than too many. If this is not handled with care, in such conditions, Game Changers can be demoralized. All too often, Game Changers know that they are not driving the impact and results that they are capable of because there is no space beyond the status quo.

There is no doubt that innovation and creativity need both time and intellectual freedom to blossom. There is an abundance of research on creativity and innovation because companies must differentiate themselves in the marketplace. The research aims to identify what characterizes "super creatives," those highly creative people who have a high tendency to see the world differently and deliver game-changing ideas. The research also shows that super creatives are risk-taking, persistent, and passionately committed people. They are Game Changers.

No matter what domain, genius ideas are formed through a continuous process that takes a certain amount of space and time. The creative flash of inspiration is therefore just the end point of a longer process of development and innovation that would be hard to imagine without flexibility, intellectual freedom, and the ability to explore.

Therefore, it is important to consciously give your Game Changers this time to think. You can trust that they will make good use of such freedom, using the flexibility that you offer to think unconventionally about existing solutions and systems. But you do this in a way that does not create an imbalance in the team's spirit. Let's explore these specific sparring skills further.

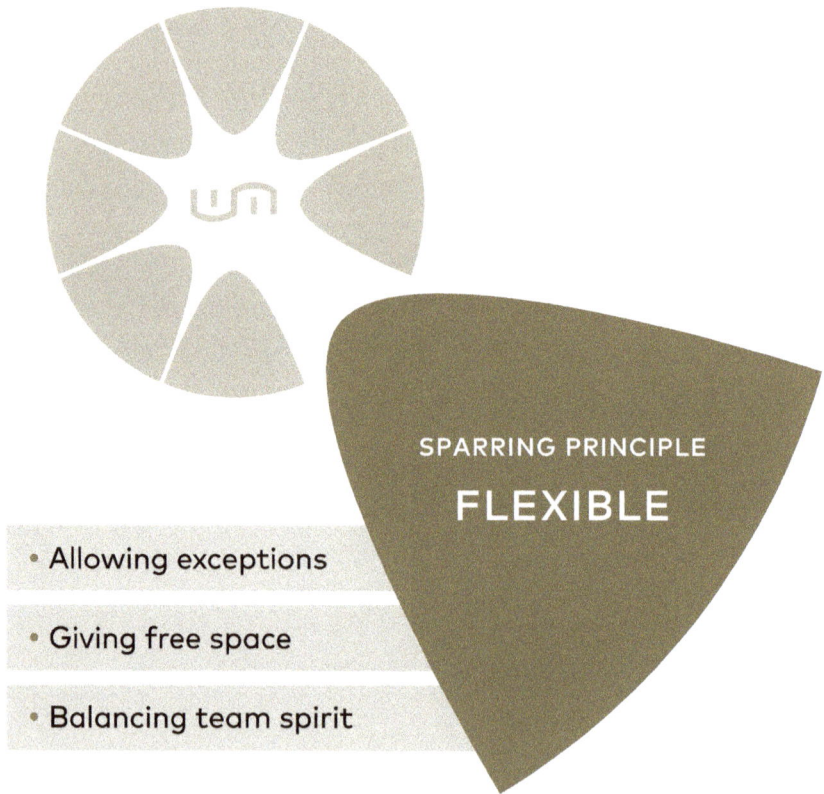

Fig. 3: The sparring principle FLEXIBLE.

Allowing Exceptions

As much as companies want to adopt standardized approaches, there are valid reasons for deviating from the standard procedures when it comes to Game Changers. This applies not only to the recruitment process and development measures, but also when staffing important key positions. Give yourself the room to decide on a case-by-case basis. Assessment centers, human resources tools, and recruitment processes are constantly evolving and ensure the quality of employee recruitment and development. However, if you are dealing with Game Changers, these methods should not be the only ones you use. To keep these top-class employees at the company in the long run, they will need more.

This may require a fundamental paradigm shift. Where in a more traditional model, Game Changers would have to adapt to the organization to truly unlock value, now the organization has to adapt, or at least meet them somewhere halfway. As a Leadership Champion, it is up to you to recognize the extraordinary potential of Game Changers and think of the long-term added value they may bring to you and your company. Similar to a great coach in sports, a Leadership Champion does not simply apply a given program, but is bold enough to allow something more individual to meet the specific needs of their Game Changer. The second sparring skill of flexibility—giving free space—fits in with this.

Giving Free Space

Giving free space is about giving Game Changers time for creativity and the space and empowerment to use their initiative so that they can best apply their talents and potential. Those who are meant to achieve out-of-the-ordinary acts have considerably better chances if they have a great level of possible freedoms. In this regard, you should also not formulate too rigid objectives. Firm SMART goals—specific, measurable, achievable, relevant, and time-bound—can be a great framework for managing performance, but do not necessarily inspire Game Changers to think big. The breaking of potentially limiting thinking patterns, however, should have a prominent place in your sparring. It is not uncommon for seemingly absurd first thoughts to grow in clarity and applicability through productive sparring.

It is in this way that Leadership Champions provide their Game Changers with the space to pursue and develop new ideas. That's because Leadership Champions are willing to create special opportunities for Game Changers to successfully execute their high-impact activities. To do this, you need to be able to adapt rigid internal rules and systems at key moments. What exactly could this mean? You could, for instance, increase budgets and decision-making powers, or remove bureaucratic hurdles and personnel restrictions to give your Game Changers additional free space and leeway that they can use to drive outstanding business success.

Balancing Team Spirit

Of course, if you grant your Game Changers exceptions and give them more free space than other team members, the rest of the team may start to take note. Since many people tend to constantly compare themselves with others, it is not uncommon for employees to get the impression that a manager may have favorites, and this almost always has negative consequences for the team's spirit. As a Leadership Champion, you are aware of this and intentionally balance it in sparring. You work with your Game Changers beyond the achievement of excellent performances, but also help them develop the ability to behave like real team players, to be socially intelligent, to stay humble, and to act modestly.

In this way, Game Changers can have a hugely positive impact on the whole team. But you need to remind them regularly to show up and to remain grounded, humble, and connected to others. As a Leadership Champion, make it your mission to make Game Changers aware of their special responsibility toward other members of their team and the team spirit.

Let's look at an example of when flexibility led to a great outcome.

Sarah

Companies in especially regulated industries are not exactly known for easily making exceptions to the rule. So, I was especially impressed by a global financial service provider who hired a promising candidate without having a job for her. How did this happen, and why would they make this unexpected choice?

The new hire, Sarah, was one of my clients who had carved out an impressive career in a different industry in just a few years. She wanted to move to another city for personal reasons, but her company could not offer her a position in that location, and they were not prepared to transition the role to being entirely remote. It seemed like a change of industry was inevitable.

Through her network, Sarah was able to connect with an executive at a financial service provider in her new hometown and have productive discussions. It was clear to the executive that Sarah had an exceptionally high level of passion, drive, and leadership experience, and that she had distinguished herself in her previous role. But Sarah was lacking financial industry experience, and this was listed as requirement number one on practically all of the company's job descriptions. On the other hand, he saw Sarah's game-changer potential and identified unique approaches that many of the industry insiders lacked.

The executive made Sarah the following offer: "You are exactly the kind of person that we are looking for, even if you are coming from a different industry. Unfortunately, we currently do not have a free position at your level. However, we can offer to create a position at a slightly lower level to give you time and support to get grounded in our industry. But I assure you that you will be promoted to the next level at the first opportunity, which we now estimate will be in eighteen months."

Sarah agreed. She dove into this new challenge, pushing herself to quickly learn the ins and outs of financial services and worked hard to build her internal network. The senior executive who hired Sarah gave her a demanding assignment right away:

To design a new version of the organization to maximize efficiencies and to drive greater innovation. He was aware that there might be some who might doubt Sarah's expertise, being a relative newcomer to the industry, and with not much time in the company. In their sparring sessions, he gave her free space to do the deep work necessary to come up with an exceptional proposal. Furthermore, he let her know that she had to approach the team members in a humble and emotionally smart way to first get respect and build relationships before voicing potentially disruptive ideas.

Soon after, Sarah had to navigate some challenging interpersonal moments, having become aware of her reputation as being the "favorite" of the senior executive. There was some resentment that she had been given such a high level of responsibility so shortly after joining. But since she had put relationship building at the top of her priority list, investing time in connecting with all members of the team with a spirit of openness and humility paid off. Soon, Sarah had built a trusted circle of colleagues who recognized her passion, commitment, and unique perspective. They were eager to work with her, and when she brought forth the new organizational design, they were ready to support her in bringing it to life.

The company kept its word, and in eighteen months, after a very successful implementation of her organizational redesign, she was promoted. Now she holds a top position and has helped the company redesign some other key business areas. Although they deviated from their usual hiring procedures, they were able to seize the opportunity to hire an exceptional talent, even if Sarah's unconventional qualifications didn't match the standard job description. It paid off. It has been a massive win-win.

#3 DEMANDING:
Productive Discomfort
Instead of Harmony

If you take a look back at your career and maybe even your life up to now, you will probably realize that it was often the particularly demanding phases that pushed you further and advanced your professional development and personal growth. When you are in the middle of such a phase, however, it often feels difficult and painful. The challenges that you have to tackle may seem so huge that you feel close to being overwhelmed. And yet, most often, it is in these times that you grow, make significant progress, and push your limits further.

Game Changers will only reach their full potential if they are led into such challenging spheres. I am convinced of this and apply this a lot in my coaching. It is the stretch mandates, assignments and goals that lead to development and more extraordinary growth in the long run.

There is an important concept by psychologist and happiness researcher Mihály Csíkszentmihályi that he refers to as "flow." This is the absorption in an activity that takes place when the demands of a challenge or task and one's abilities correlate adequately. As a result, flow is a state of highest concentration, in which the execution of one's activities is experienced as enjoyable because you almost lose yourself in it, become completely in the moment, very productive, and totally connected. If, on the other hand, your skills are greater than the requirements of a task, it soon may become too easy, too routine, and boredom arises. And if the requirements of a challenge exceed your capabilities, you are challenged above the flow zone, resulting in you experiencing discomfort and stretch, and maybe even at risk of being overstretched.

Leadership Champions should strive for their employees to create the framework so that everyone can experience this flow regularly when the requirements of a task are brought into an optimal relationship with the skills and capabilities of the individuals. In the flow, they can achieve a lot, and at the same time, they feel very good about their personal experience when delivering their performance. However, you need to consistently and deliberately adapt this system, especially for your Game Changers. That's because over time, their abilities will outgrow the specific demands of a certain challenge. They will first experience a form of ease and comfort. Later, this will move into boredom. Therefore, to increase their performance level and continue to maximize their impact, Game Changers must face challenges that are more difficult than what they can currently manage in the flow. And there is a certain necessary discomfort in this shift.

The above-the-flow channel is the zone where a task requires the utmost effort because it demands the development and application of new thinking, skills, capabilities, or approaches to succeed. We can call this area the development zone (see Figure 4). If athletes never leave their flow state, they would most likely remain successful but at a mediocre level. And then get bored because they would be missing an adequate new challenge. Imagine a tennis player who regularly wins mid-level tournaments but never moves on to compete in major tournaments. This would be unimaginable for Game Changers because they know that in order to learn and develop, one must experience discomfort. The same principle applies to business.

FLOW CHANNEL DIAGRAM

Development takes place outside the flow channel

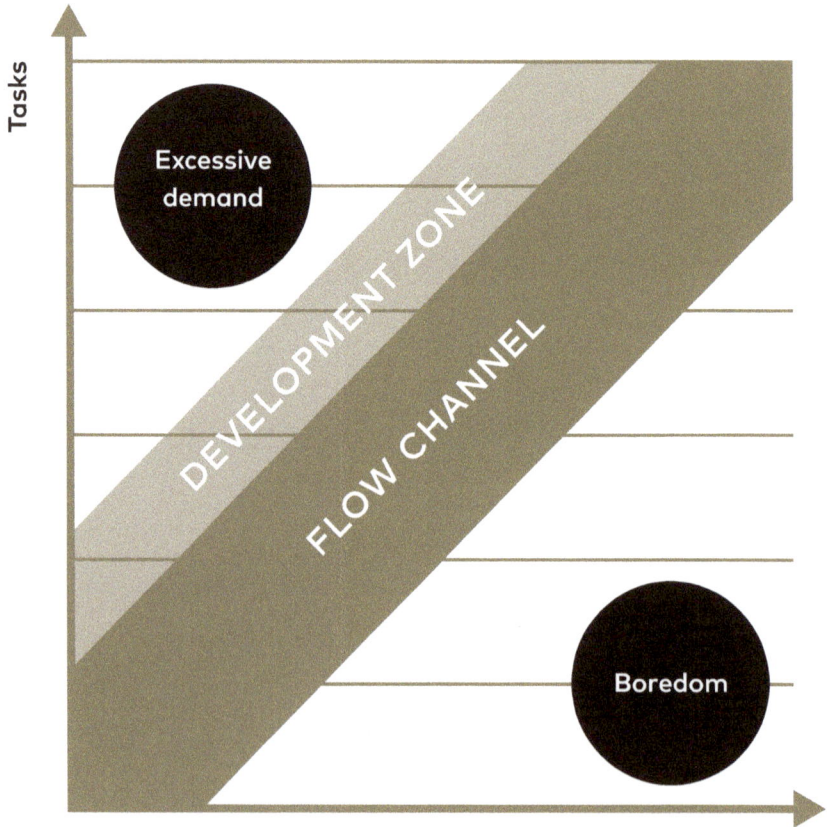

Fig. 4: The Development Zone (following Csíkszentmihályi).

Whether it's taking up a new job, a senior leadership assignment, or a transformative change project for the first time, none of these can be managed completely within the flow channel, and yet each of these steps are necessary to develop a new level of exceptional performance. What I regularly notice is that Game Changers not only commit to continuous development, but because of their desire for input and feedback and their ability to transform input into action, they tend to master new challenges faster than their peers. It is because of their higher-than-average level of passion and mental toughness that they can shoulder greater responsibilities in a shorter time frame.

Therefore, as a Leadership Champion, you can intentionally challenge your Game Changers, be demanding, and expect more of them than you do of others.

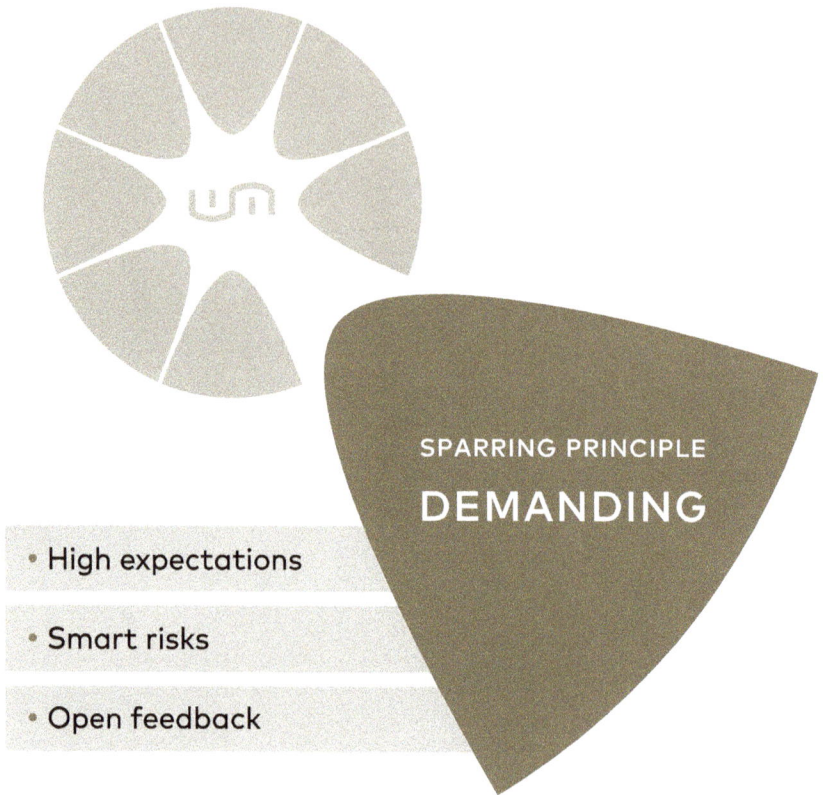

Fig. 5: The sparring principle DEMANDING.

High Expectations

Game Changers develop and grow primarily through experience, taking on tasks that are very demanding for them. Where this development zone begins is different for each person and changes constantly over the course of a career. The better you, as a Leadership Champion, know and understand your Game Changers, the more solidly you can assess the specific possibilities and opportunities for their development. In other words, the more willing you are as a Leadership Champion to truly engage with your Game Changers, the more you will be able to specifically shape the course for their optimal development. The foundation of this development work is the setting of high expectations.

So, what does this mean in real time? Articulate your high expectations to your Game Changers and intentionally make these expectations slightly higher than their actual capability and specific to certain tasks and situations. The point is not to introduce constant unnecessary pressure or stress. You are intentionally asking your Game Changers to stretch forward, but temporarily and in a targeted manner. You should never permanently push your Game Changer beyond their stress limit. Otherwise, they might burn out from constant overwhelm, which must be avoided at all costs.

Smart Risks

Big challenges and high expectations always carry a big risk: The risk of failure. With this in mind, we need to acknowledge that there is a narrow line between demanding and asking too much. The rigorous aspect of sparring is not an easy thing for a Leadership Champion. In the end, you, just like your Game Changers, cannot be absolutely sure that when you push your Game Changers to take on a new, particularly challenging task that it will result in success.

As discussed, the final decision and accountability in sparring should be with the Game Changer. Therefore, like Game Changers, Leadership Champions also leave safe ground behind and consciously take smart, controlled risks to achieve the best possible overarching outcomes. Therefore, you need to evaluate carefully, take the broad view, and consider all the different dimensions of the challenge, staying close and re-evaluating them regularly. Take smart risks, but never set your Game Changers up for failure with blind risks.

Open Feedback

Openness is a core element in sparring. When things get difficult, openness becomes twice as important. High-quality feedback is honest and no-frills, and in a relationship that is marked by trust, there is the necessary space to tell each other unpleasant truths in a respectful manner.

Make regular feedback moments a systematic part of your sparring. Be obsessed with identifying various occasions to gather inputs that you can share in your sparring systematically. It can happen in key meetings, during customer discussions, or in important presentations.

Sparring demands the ability to bear it when things aren't that harmonious. After all, sparring thrives on two strong partners who openly engage to find the best possible solution. Differences in opinion can and should be regularly aired and explored. Here's how this plays out in real life:

Max

Max was going through an extensive process of interviews and external assessments before he was offered the CFO position at a large technology company. The position was sought after by many of his peers, but there had been several leadership changes recently—three different CFOs in four years had many wondering what was going on and why continuity was so challenging. Max was excited about this role, but with such a bumpy history, he knew he was in for a massive challenge.

After a few weeks in the role, Max soon realized why his predecessors had never been able to hold on to the position for long: Team members worked more against each other than with, and were not motivated to come together. Max's mission was, therefore, not only to reliably process complex data and provide decision-making foundations for the CEO, the executive team, and the board. But to also readjust the dysfunctional team, partly re-staff it, communicate a compelling vision, give constructive feedback as an inspiring manager, fight against demotivation, and, at times, compensate for poorly executed work. If Max couldn't readjust the team dynamics, he risked continued infighting and poor performance. That's because it wasn't an option to simply reorganize the team and hire new people.

Thankfully, the CEO knew about the scale of the challenge and how much leadership would be required to address many of the issues at the root cause. Wanting to make sure that Max was set up for success, the CEO organized regular sparring meetings with him. The CEO's focus was to set high expectations, while at the same time giving Max the backup he needed to stretch to the very high demands of the role. Max appreciated that he wasn't left alone to navigate the challenging dynamics of the role, but had a Leadership Champion who was generous in sharing his experience and insights, who helped him to understand the context, and visibly showed his trust in him to his peers in the executive team.

An important topic in the sparring discussions was around what it meant to take smart risks. Max got the message that he was not expected to just keep things running optimally, build a better team dynamic, and keep things stable. Rather, the CEO wanted him to push further, to challenge the status quo, take smart risks, and mine for innovative ideas, even those that were yet unproven, and contribute significantly to the growth of the company. That's because in the highly competitive tech world, keeping things stable was the same as taking a step backward. They needed to unlock innovation in every area of the business, particularly in finance, to stay competitive.

In their sparring sessions, Max soon learned that his CEO was not shying away from open feedback. He addressed, timely and truthfully, when Max did not perform well. At the beginning, after such pointed sparring sessions, Max was wary that he wasn't living up to the CEO's expectations. But on the other hand, he had no reason to doubt the trust the CEO had placed in him. Max soon recognized what a gift the CEO was giving him by taking the time to check in, give him open and honest feedback, and provide the push he needed at critical moments while fundamentally backing him up.

All in all, Max did not have an easy start. But after eight months, Max was on solid footing, leading his team with confidence and clarity toward a clearly articulated, new and ambitious strategy. This was key to greater team cohesion and a much stronger sense of shared purpose. In doing this, Max was able to turn the page on the challenging history of the finance function and regain the confidence of his peers in the executive team.

Max has now been CFO for three years, and the company has significantly grown with two back-to-back record years on all financial key performance indicators.

#4 MAXIMALLY SUPPORTIVE:
Clearing the Path Instead
of Delivering Fixes

The modern world of business is often so complex that decisions have to be made based on insufficient or incomplete information, under time pressure, in new contexts, and in constantly changing environments. This makes sparring an ideal instrument for Leadership Champions to help Game Changers stress test various scenarios.

Game Changers, however, can unleash their full potential only when the high demands and expectations set on them are combined with maximal support from their Leadership Champion. When a Game Changer can rely on the full support of their Leadership Champion, especially during such intense periods and stress tests, it will strengthen their relationship immensely and create the foundation for a successful, outstanding long-term cooperation. But this is only possible if both sides have built up so much trust in each other that they can share their worries or even fears, admit mistakes, and acknowledge their momentary discomfort. It is this openness and vulnerability that will enable you, as the Leadership Champion, to become the most effective sparring partner you can be.

You can maximize your support as a Leadership Champion on many levels. Let's take a closer look at these different types of support, from cognitive to emotional to practical.

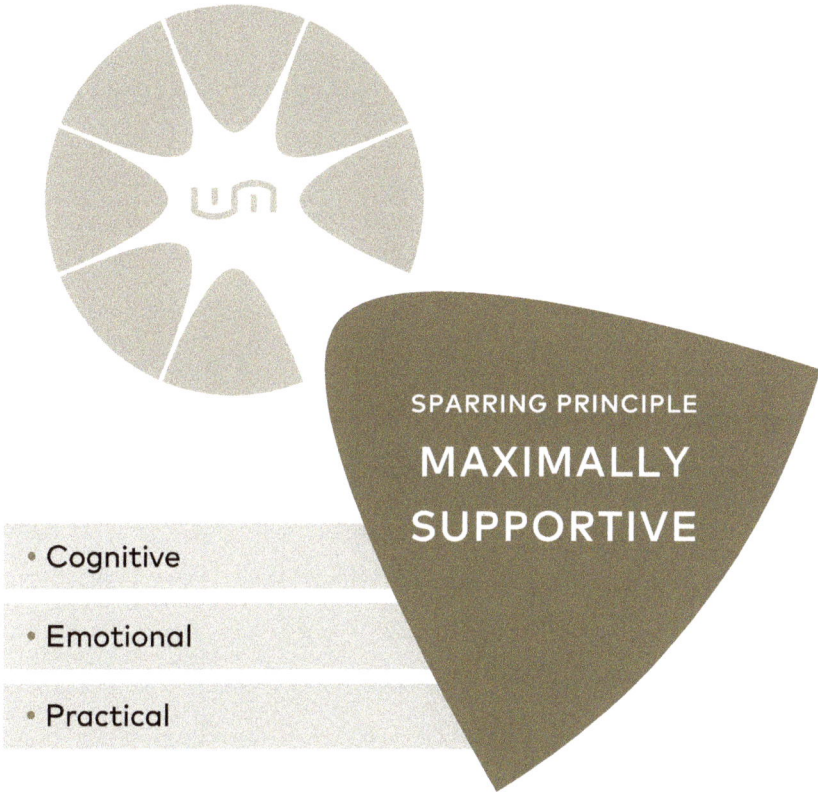

SPARRING PRINCIPLE

MAXIMALLY
SUPPORTIVE

- Cognitive

- Emotional

- Practical

Fig. 6: The sparring principle MAXIMALLY SUPPORTIVE.

Cognitive Support

Cognitive support means assisting your Game Changers with rational insights, expertise, research, and recommendations, as well as discussing a problem and providing your very deep knowledge and experience. One example would be when a Leadership Champion shines a light on unwritten rules that might be difficult for a newcomer to decode, or directs them to some resources or research that might offer useful insights or approaches. Cognitive support plays an important role when sparring about ideas and arguments. As a Leadership Champion, you should offer all of your expertise—such as analytical thinking, logical judgment, or knowledge based on reason and objectivity—to optimally support your Game Changers in finding breakthrough solutions.

Emotional Support

This type of support can be thought of as encouragement that makes it easier for the other person to successfully manage a difficult situation. Typical signs of support are: "I stand behind you," "I am convinced that you can manage this," or "If there is something you need, you can rely on me." Emotional support gives your Game Changer confidence by knowing that you back them up and can be highly relevant to their performance.

Effective emotional support requires a relationship built on trust, as well as being able to empathize with what the Game Changer is experiencing. As a Leadership Champion, you should directly address the emotional state of your Game Changer when working on a particularly challenging topic. Some examples include: "How are you feeling about this project?" "What feelings come to you when you think about this challenge?" "How would you feel if you were to execute the decision?"

Only those who feel understood and respected in their opinions and emotions are really ready to take a bold next step and embrace smart risks with confidence and determination. In this way, you convey the feeling of solidarity and a shared mission, which helps them execute with high self-confidence and, therefore, a high chance of success.

Practical Support

This type of support requires you to concretely unburden a Game Changer through pragmatic help, such as temporarily taking over some of a Game Changer's tasks, or providing additional resources or services. In this way, practical support enables Game Changers to devote themselves entirely to a demanding task. In short, this is the classic lightening of someone's load.

Here's a real-life example: The head of a legal department, who, at the critical stage of the Europe-wide implementation of new data protection directives, largely relieved his dedicated leadership team member of other day-to-day business. The Leadership Champion told the Game Changer, "For the next eight weeks, you should concentrate fully on the implementation of the new rules. Pass all other legal requests and projects on to me."

However, this form of practical support may surprise some executives. But it makes sense for a Leadership Champion to take work off their Game Changers' plates in certain situations. This has nothing to do with having tasks delegated back to you. It is much more about clearing the path and giving Game Changers, under particularly demanding conditions, the practical support to concentrate fully on their most important task and to complete it successfully. Such leadership behavior is even more effective because the gleam of success at the end shines on the Game Changer and less so on yourself, even if you significantly contributed to the success by clearing the path. This is exactly what distinguishes Leadership Champions at their core: They make sure that their people achieve great success in the interest of the company, through their leadership.

Here's an example of when maximal support made a huge difference.

Matthias

Matthias successfully presented his analysis of the existing data and strategic plan to the technical committee of his corporation. In the last few months, he had invested a lot of time into the preparation of the presentation, knowing how important it was for the strategic direction of the company. There was a new opportunity coming up on the horizon, and the committee relied on Matthias's thorough assessment of its commercial potential. He was confident and happy that most of his recommendations were picked up by the committee.

But during the weeks following his presentation, doubts crept in. Had he really succeeded in taking all the right parameters into account and in doing so created the comprehensive foundation for the committee's decision-making? At last, it became clear to Matthias that he had made a mistake. Matthias had not given enough weight to the data source that initially seemed not to be relevant during his analysis.

Matthias gave this data a deeper examination and concluded that the data was more relevant than he initially assessed. In fact, he should have weighed it more in his recommendations.

Matthias turned to me for advice. After we had discussed various scenarios, he decided to ask for a sparring conversation with his manager, the Global Commercial Head (GCH) of the company. In their sparring, they discussed the pros and cons of different approaches. It was a very demanding situation for Matthias, who openly admitted his mistake. He had to hope that his boss would not seek to cast blame and scapegoat, but would instead appreciate his honesty.

Together, the GCH and Matthias concluded on the following: They would go back to the committee as soon as possible to explain the situation and to lay out the updated analysis with the subsequent recommendations. In the meantime, Matthias received very concrete insights and support from his manager on how to specifically articulate the mistake in a constructive way in front of the committee. Furthermore, he assured Matthias that he would back him up, that he would protect him in case of negative reactions from the committee. He said, "I will tell them that I am accountable," and took all the other tasks from Matthias and temporarily delegated them to the other team members so that Matthias could focus entirely on the new analysis and presentation before the upcoming meeting with the committee.

What transpired was game-changing for the company: Transparently admitting what had happened and course-correcting immediately was highly appreciated by the committee and contributed even further to an atmosphere of trust and accountability, which was fully in line with the company's values. Most importantly, the strategic decision was revised, and the new recommendation led to a massive success. The company was the first in its market to offer an innovative new product to its customers, which has been in high demand ever since.

#5 PLAYFUL:
Light-Footed Instead
of Heavy-Handed

When hearing about high performance, very often it is assumed it relies mostly on discipline, will-power, and perseverance. In short, high performance is often talked about as hard work and heavy lifting. Many idioms and maxims also make that connection. "No pain, no gain" or "Genius is 1 percent inspiration and 99 percent perspiration" are widely known as secrets for success. Of course, sustainable high-performance and extraordinary results do not come without persistent efforts and ongoing commitment. But this view alone is too narrow.

Looking back at my years working in top-level sports, I know for sure that it is no coincidence that the athletes who make it to the top very seldom produce high performance without a form of joy and playfulness. Playfulness, or the ability to tackle hard things in a light way, is critical to perseverance and to the ability to be at your best when it counts. However, only those who master their craft and have the necessary elements in place can be playful.

Likewise, in business, it is crucial to transform the obsession for winning into something more playful, to allow for lightness and ease, and to make playful energy more commonplace on the highest level over time. Playfulness means not taking everything so seriously that it becomes counterproductive or draining. Think about it. How much fun do people have in your teams? How often do they laugh? If you consider such questions as absurd and insist on focusing solely on what's accomplished through hard work and grinding rather than on opportunities for more strategic ease, read this section closely. In the long run, your people do not work better under constant pressure, threats, or fear of failure. That only makes them work with more anxiety. It may mobilize some focus in the short term, but it will not inspire creativity and winning innovation.

One may argue that high performers can handle pressure and stress well. In fact, in the first part of this book, I discuss how mental toughness, the ability to handle high-pressure situations and to successfully overcome them, is one of the defining characteristics of Game Changers. But permanent high pressure in an overall negative context wears down even the strongest people. Laughter, humor, and fun are release valves to discharge stress in difficult situations. As a Leadership Champion, you can role model a sense of productive light-hearted-ness for your teams.

Similarly, sparring is strenuous, demanding, and not always harmonious. But it also needs a dose of lightness to maintain the Game Changer's confidence. This is why I consider the fifth sparring principle to be playful. My core conviction is this: For Game Changers to approach challenges open and playfully, you, as the Leadership Champion, must radiate a confident, optimistic, and upbeat attitude and lead by example, demonstrating that high performance and lightness can go hand in hand.

Let's look at the skills of the playful sparring principle one by one.

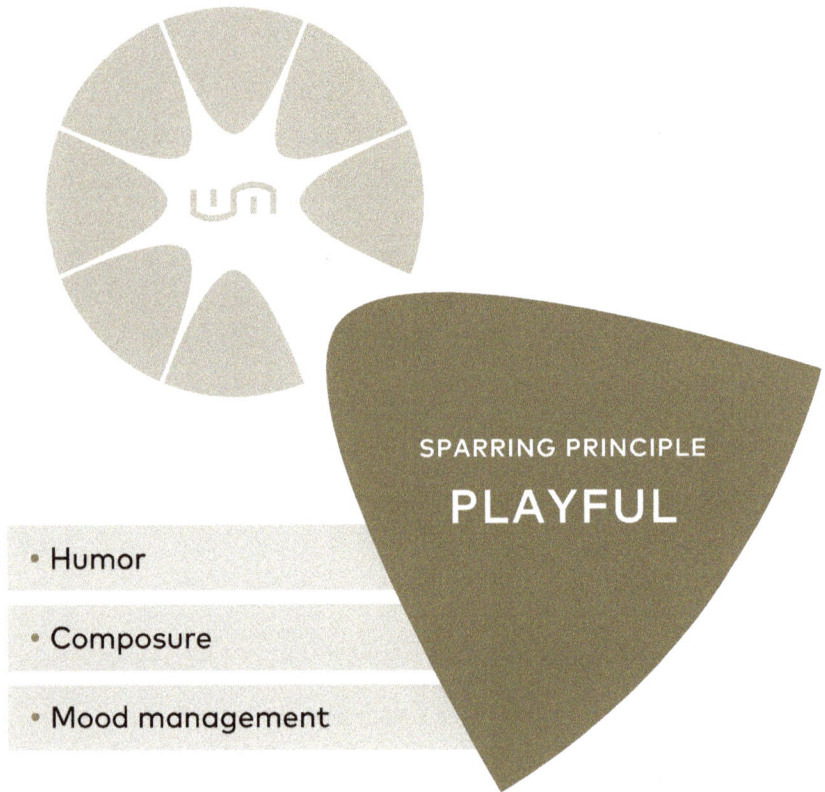

Fig. 7: The sparring principle PLAYFUL.

Humor

Humor is the ability to see situations in a different context that offers distance from the events, revealing a funny or even silly side of the matter. It helps people manage their ability to act even in intense circumstances. I find positive humor works best as sarcasm, devaluations, jokes at the expense of others, and similar forms of aggressive humor have the opposite effect. Why? Because they may add strain to the working environment and create further pressure. Use humor to lessen pressure, not increase it.

The real power of positive humor is its ability to help us reveal more of our authentic selves and become more approachable. That's because dry one-liners, self-irony, puns, and comic exaggeration in good fun are funniest when they are personal. In turn, this healthy playfulness allows others to connect on a more human level. The united front of all forms of positive humor is the attitude behind it: Not to take yourself and the situation so seriously that it limits your ability to act.

Shared laughter connects people and can be considered healthy as well. Have you ever noticed or felt more alert and relaxed after a hearty laugh? Laughter not only produces endorphins and lowers your level of adrenaline, but it also stretches the lungs, increases the oxygen concentration in your blood, and stimulates your metabolism. Laughter even strengthens the immune system.

Take advantage of the relaxing effects of humor and consciously choose to take a humorous view on a situation. Especially when the overall situation appears to be difficult, when great challenges have to be dealt with, and the pressure feels overwhelming. A well-placed sense of humor can help enormously as long as you do not forget reality. Because, of course, laughter doesn't actually solve a problem. It makes a problem easier to bear.

Composure

Have you ever worked with a leader who was constantly tense and stressed-out? Then you would agree that tension is transferable. That's how bad moods take root in teams and spread. We can enter a room and sense without a word being spoken if there is trouble brewing because we immediately feel uncomfortable.

Luckily, this effect also works the other way around. Positive feelings, vibes, and moods are similarly infectious. That is why more people smile at us whenever we are having a really good day. Neurologists and memory psychologists attribute this effect to so-called mirror neurons that work as amplifiers in the brain. For our context of leadership, and the sparring necessary for a Winning Match, this means that if you, as a Leader Champion, radiate warm, calm composure, you create the best foundation for an engaged, solution-oriented, and creative discussion with your Game Changers. That's because being composed means acting with confidence, while being highly concentrated, optimistic for a positive outcome, and focused at the same time. When you can physically translate the feeling: "We'll get there, we'll make it," you take the potentially destructive pressure out of the situation, and your Game Changers will very likely take on the same composed attitude.

Mood Management

As a Leadership Champion, you are ready to take any unnecessary heaviness out of a situation for your people, your teams, and especially for your Game Changers, even more so when a lot of pressure has built up. That's because you know how important it is to actively raise their spirits.

If you take the time to favorably influence the mood and atmosphere at pivotal moments, upcoming challenges will look far less difficult and will not reach the level of threat. In addition to humor and calm composure, you can manage and positively influence the mood of others with well-chosen words and language. Your speech can convey a soothing ease that will help your Game Changers take on challenging tasks far more easily.

Let's learn more by taking a look at another one of my coaching examples.

Damian

Together with one of my clients, Damian, a member of the executive team of a leading global infrastructure company, I conducted a multi-day mentoring program to take place twice a year. Damian and his leadership team selected key talents to undergo a leadership mentoring experience that I had specifically designed for them. Damian was excited about the program. He referred to its impact, and in previous deliveries, was highly engaged and present, networking with all of the participants as almost a master of ceremonies. Damian brought his passion and enthusiasm to the room, which positively impacted the mood and created a strong sense of energy among the participants.

When we were planning for the next cohort, I didn't know that the program fell right in the middle of the last phase of an important company acquisition, since it was highly confidential. I only learned later, when it became public, that Damian was responsible for the deal after a challenging negotiation that had a real risk of not going through.

During the program, there were a few moments when Damian seemed a bit distracted. When I asked him if he needed me to support him in any additional way, he said, "Yes, you're right. I could use a little bit of extra support." He then asked me to run specific parts of the program without him, and of course, I was happy to help. The participants quickly noticed that Damian was stepping out and was on the phone quite often, but he managed to drop in from time to time, and each time injected great substance, a strong dose of energy, and positivity into the group.

During the sessions he participated in, Damian was as present and as constructive as always, showing a strong sense of interest in his people, with keen questions and observations, and even bringing positive humor and a sense of lightness when the group struggled with a difficult concept.

Even though he also had to take calls during the breaks, Damian stayed close to the session's agenda. He then asked me to make some shifts to the agenda so that even though he would have to leave early, he would not miss a chance to thank the participants, to share some motivating words, and to tell them how excited he was to continue on this development journey together.

During his closing speech, Damian apologized for having to leave early, thanked everyone involved, and added with a smile, "As some of you know, we have been in the middle of negotiations with a top player in our market about a hot acquisition. I am now finally allowed to speak about it as it materialized this week. During the last few days, my day job was being here with you at the program, while I worked nights and coffee breaks on the company acquisition. It was one of these weeks with a day job and a night job. But this program is so important for me that I had to make sure I could be here as much as possible. I was pulled in a lot of different directions to say the least, I hope you couldn't tell too much!"

The participants were blown away. They felt honored that Damian kept his commitment to them during such a pivotal and high-stakes moment for the company. But even though he had to prioritize a mission-critical negotiation, Damian also stayed with them on their development journey as much as possible. He asked me to do even more parts of the program, which was absolutely no problem for me, and trusted that they were in good hands. Damian also took care to make sure that when he was there, he was all in and fully present with the group.

As always, Damian was a major driver of the program's success. In a truly impressive way, he delivered an absolute top performance on both fronts—the acquisition and the program's impact. Damian was a role model for grace and lightness under pressure thanks to his composure and playfulness.

LEADERSHIP CHAMPIONS
AT A GLANCE

The success of the Winning Match model demands a specific type of leadership. Let's summarize the key qualities of Leadership Champions once again:

- Game Changer Scouting Skills

- Ambition for Overarching Success

- Maximum Unconditional Generosity, and the desire to have a lasting, positive effect on others

- Sparring Capabilities with the Principles: Respectful, Flexible, Demanding, Maximally Supportive, and Playful

Figure 8 summarizes the characteristics of Leadership Champions at a glance.

WINNING MATCH

Leadership Champion

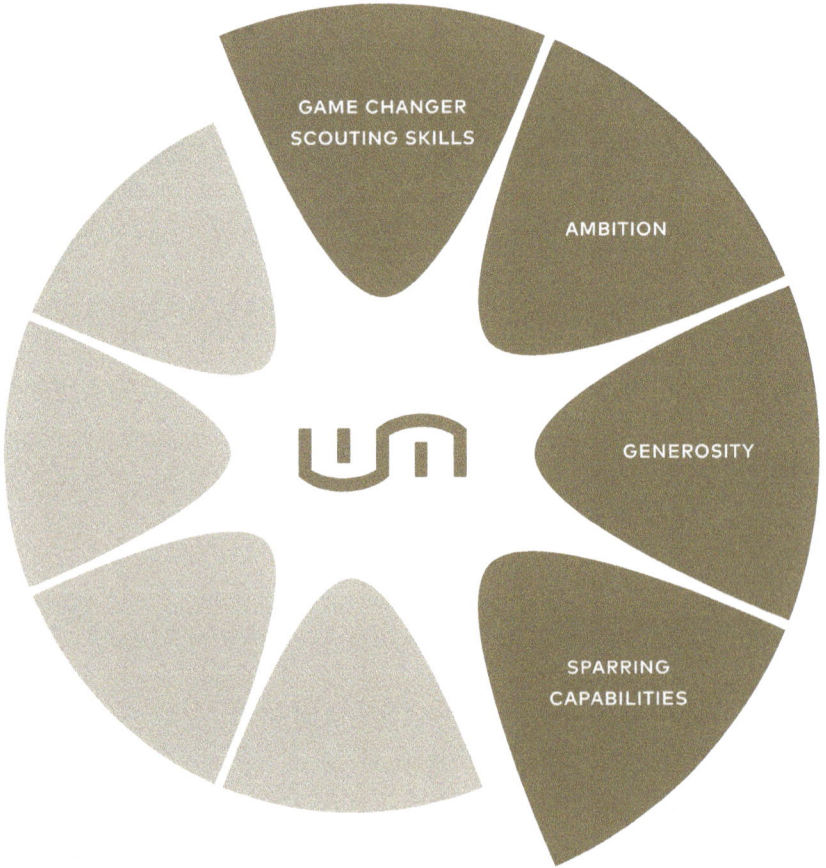

GAME CHANGER
SCOUTING SKILLS

AMBITION

GENEROSITY

SPARRING
CAPABILITIES

Fig. 8: Characteristics of Leadership Champions at a glance.

THE WINNING MATCH MODEL

So far, I have dealt with the key characteristics of Game Changers and Leadership Champions.

In a nutshell, Leadership Champions are ambitious but not egocentric leaders who put themselves at the service of the corporation's overarching success and their Game Changers, aiming to have a lasting, positive impact. Leadership Champions develop an effective sparring competence and optimally support their Game Changers in their personal development and in their ability to push the boundaries.

Game changers are characterized by a high degree of passion. They feel strongly committed to their organization's mission and purpose, to their tasks, contributions, and their performance to the highest possible level, and have a strong desire for high-quality input and feedback. They have a great ability to transform input into action and the mental toughness to make great things happen.

WINNING MATCH

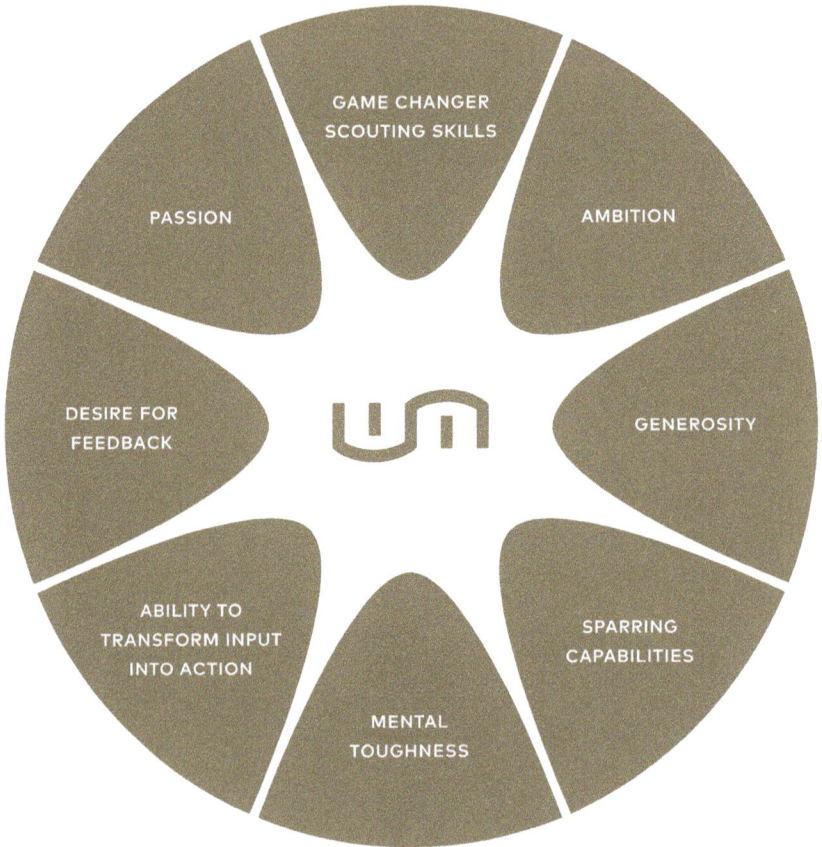

Fig. 9: The Winning Match model.
On the left: The Characteristics of Game Changers;
On the right: The Characteristics of Leadership Champions.

In the next part of this book, I will focus on the Winning Match model in practice. Let's turn our attention to the moments when you will make the best even better.

PART III

WINNING MATCH MOMENTS

THE SPECIAL MAGIC
IN A WINNING MATCH

The pairing of a Game Changer with a Leadership Champion is where the magic starts to happen in a Winning Match, ultimately leading to long-term and sustainable, positive impact for the company.

How does a Winning Match function in the day-to-day course of business? When do the sparring principles come into play? How can you use its power in Winning Match moments? Thankfully, top-tier sports give us valuable clues. The interaction between great coaches and athletes begins first in the regular day-to-day training and the constant optimization and polishing of even the smallest details. This provides an important foundation. But sports training isn't just trying to achieve peak conditioning. It is also about preparing for competition and key decisive performance moments. Ultimately, it is a steady buildup to ensure overall readiness for top performance, particularly when circumstances are adverse or cannot be fully controlled or predicted.

Together, athletes and their coaches gain new, ground-breaking insights in those decisive moments, and this can lead to a breakthrough in their collaboration. It may come with defeat, which brings the coach and the athlete together, looking for the root causes and working out ways to adapt the approach. It may come with victory, whereby it is crucial to analyze the conditions and what worked well in the athlete's performance to make it repeatable. Such milestones, when a new level is reached, represent the essence of Winning Match moments. This is where the intense sparring between the two reaches its full impact.

It is the same in business when I observe a Leadership Champion and a Game Changer operating together in top form. A strong professional relationship built on closeness and trust lays the foundation for an intensive, open exchange and paves the way for new ideas, creative solutions, and outstanding results. Yet these need to come out of specific, targeted interactions—in Winning Match moments.

The study of human motivation generally defines three general human needs: the need for social inclusion (affiliation), the need for competence (ability to act and have an impact in a given situation), and the need for autonomy (voluntary action or acting from insight, not due to external pressure). The Winning Match model addresses all three core human motivational needs. First, it creates a highly trusting working relationship—the need for bonding and inclusion. Second, through sparring, the potential and capability of Game Changers is valued and taken into account—the need for competence. And third, Leadership Champions pass on a strong degree of responsibility to their Game Changers, taking into account the need for autonomy.

Therefore, a Winning Match moment very often has a massive motivational impact on Game Changers. They realize that they can rely on their Leadership Champions, they are trusted to take on the next big challenge, and they know that they are fully supported. Ultimately, Winning Match moments boost the Game Changer's self-confidence and fuel their drive to succeed and make a meaningful impact.

.

INTENTIONALLY CREATING WINNING MATCH MOMENTS

What prerequisites are necessary for the realization of a Winning Match moment? Figure 10 illustrates that both of you, you as the Leadership Champion and your Game Changer, need to be fundamentally aligned on the following:

- Both understand the topic, challenge, task, or issue at hand, and its dimension
- Both green-light the same goals and view of optimal outcomes
- Both agree on what approaches can lead to positive solutions and outcomes
- Both envision what the sustainable pursuit of targets can look like
- Both grasp the relevance or importance of the key focus areas
- Both value the prioritization and urgency of the topic, challenge, task, or issue

WINNING MATCH MOMENT

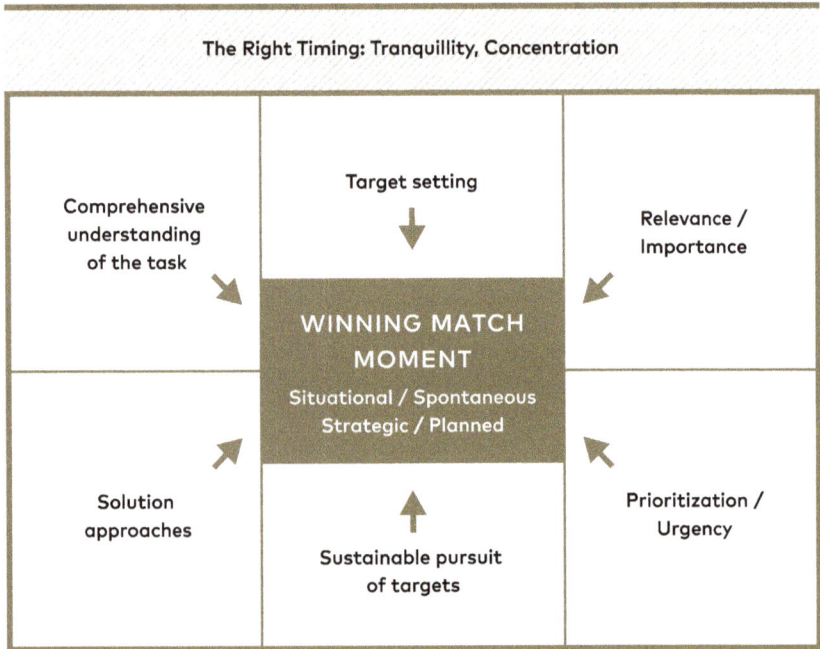

The Right Timing: Tranquillity, Concentration
Comprehensive understanding of the task	Target setting	Relevance / Importance
	WINNING MATCH MOMENT Situational / Spontaneous Strategic / Planned	
Solution approaches	Sustainable pursuit of targets	Prioritization / Urgency

Fig. 10: Requirements for Winning Match moments.

In addition, a successful Winning Match moment also requires the right timing so that both of you—the Leadership Champion and the Game Changer—are mentally and emotionally in the right place to engage in productive sparring. Only if both match partners have their heads cleared for an intense, highly productive dialogue, especially if you and your Game Changer are calm, concentrated, and receptive—ideally within a setting that offers adequate tranquility—can such moments be most effective.

In reality, Winning Match moments can arise spontaneously, out of a specific occasion, in day-to-day business. This is when you need to carve out some time ad hoc, connect with your Game Changers immediately, and create a Winning Match moment to develop a great decision for a pressing issue. Sometimes, however, it may well be the case that an emerging topic is very relevant, but the time is not yet right for an intensive sparring because another very important topic has to be dealt with first. In this case, I recommend that you postpone the sparring and deal with it later.

Planned Winning Match moments, on the other hand, are the regular sparring sessions that you can schedule for your Game Changers. The advantage of the planned sparring sessions is that both of you can prepare for these in advance, get yourselves mentally and emotionally in the right place, and follow up on the most critical themes in a structured way.

Let's look at this in a more detailed manner.

SITUATIONAL AND STRATEGIC WINNING MATCH MOMENTS

As just mentioned, Winning Match moments can arise situationally through sudden, mostly unanticipated situations, problems, or difficulties that need to be taken care of rather unexpectedly. For example, if you receive surprise results, you most often need to act immediately. Your Game Changers will be on board because they take full responsibility for their actions, and because of their desire for feedback and ability to transform input into action, they are very much interested in receiving immediate new inputs, honest feedback and developing possible solutions in sparring so that they can course correct.

Strategically induced, planned Winning Match moments are the sparring sessions that you would plan to take place every four to six weeks or more frequently if there is a higher urgency. These are planned time slots throughout the year that you both protect and prioritize. It is the time when you plan to contribute to make great things happen through your Game Changers.

The following three practical action steps can help you create Winning Match moments with your Game Changers:

- **Change the location for the sparring discussion.**

  When sparring sessions take place in the Leadership Champion's office, this can potentially reinforce the perception of a formal hierarchy. This is unfavorable for Winning Match moments. A neutral, inspiring location can help create greater openness and interactions at eye level.

- **Focus and visualize big goals.**

  These should be beyond the usual tar-get-setting cycle. Focus primarily on overarching business goals such as inno-vation, growth, or productivity, and on long-term personal development targets. If possible, visualize the desired outcome, for example, with a picture or a symbol that you can always refer to in an inspiring way. Bring it along to each sparring session to create the most positive conditions.

- **Write down topics that have been sparred about and ensure that you follow up.**

Take personal notes of the topics, decisions, and actions that result from the sparring sessions. Use this to introduce the upcoming sparring session, so you both can track and monitor progress and create and maintain a positive momentum. This way, you lay the best basis for further Winning Match moments. And keep a backlog of other important topics for future sparring sessions.

WHERE
WINNING MATCH MOMENTS
UNLOCK BUSINESS VALUE

We have covered the when and how for Winning Match moments. To bring this home: What should your sparring sessions with your Game Changers be focused on? The contents of such Winning Match moments can be very diverse. Figure 11 illustrates some of the key focus areas for you.

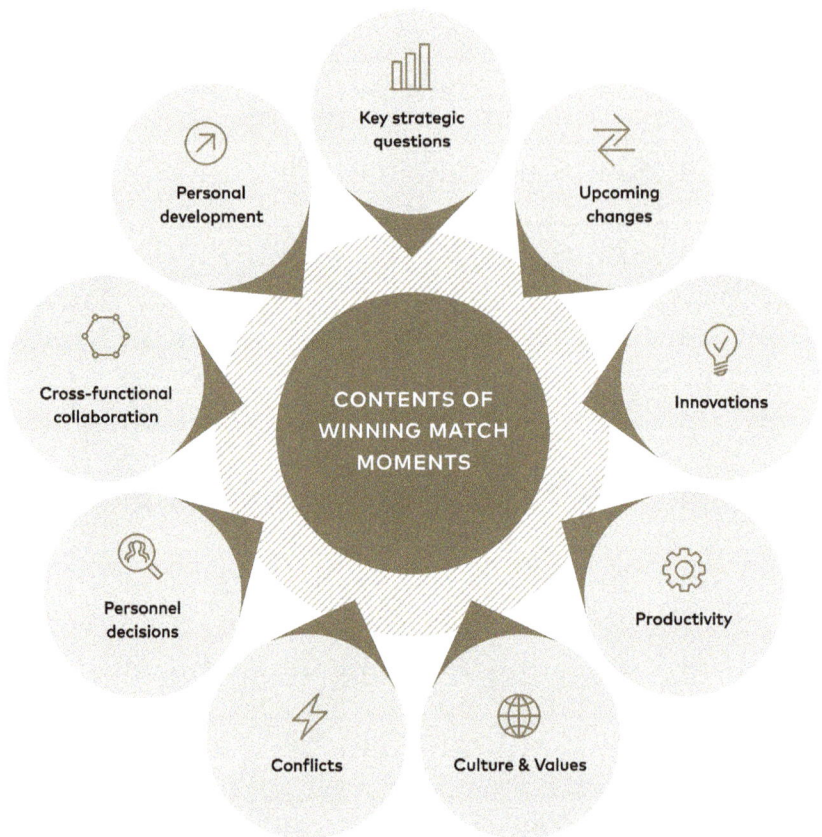

Fig. 11: Contents of Winning Match moments.

This figure shows some key areas where Winning Match moments have the potential to make a powerful impact on some of the most vital parts of the business. Let's take a closer look at the different areas where a Winning Match can be transformative.

- **Key strategic questions**

Regularly engage your Game Changers in strategic questions, for example, the future direction of a department or the entire company, acquisitions, divestments, growth, product research, and development. The list of fundamental strategic questions can be broad. Winning Match moments are the ideal catalysts for deep thinking (and re-thinking) of the business strategy.

- **Upcoming changes**

Business models and organizational structures are constantly evolving in most companies, which often goes hand-in-hand with numerous challenges that arise when the organization is asked to adapt. In order to implement changes as quickly as possible, Game Changers can identify concrete and practical measures in Winning Match moments.

- **Innovations**

The innovative power of a company significantly determines how sustainable and how successful it can be in the future. Winning Match moments are ideal because they promote the creativity of Game Changers and foster the motivation and courage to tackle new, groundbreaking ideas and put them into practice.

- **Productivity**

  Measures that increase the productivity of a company can be at the center of a Winning Match moment. You can therefore direct your sparring sessions with your Game Changers on approaches to maximize efficiency, effectiveness, and productivity.

- **Corporate culture and values**

  A successful company is most often based on a healthy, productive culture. To design the cultural framework (including the key values) or to adapt it to new conditions is an area where Winning Match moments can deliver decisive insights.

- **Conflicts**

  Even in the best team, disagreements will occur because, after all, people think and tick differently (which is good!). However, if conflicts that are potentially harming relationships are negated or suppressed, they can seriously jeopardize the success of everything. In Winning Match moments, it is possible to productively discuss the path to strengthen relationships and realign everyone to the common goals.

- **Personnel decisions**

  Personnel decisions, such as who gets hired or who gets promoted, have a massive influence on the performance of a team and ultimately of the company. Using Winning Match moments with your Game Changers to create more clarity can lead to more informed decisions.

- **Cross-functional collaboration**

  Complexity is increasing in almost every industry. A good cross-functional collaboration is, therefore, indispensable. Leadership Champions and Game Changers who bring about Winning Match moments are predestined to create synergies between functions, teams, and individuals.

- **Personal development**

  Leadership Champions have a strong interest in the growth and development of their people, especially of their Game Changers. This ranges from identifying potential blind spots in self-perception to actively supporting future career steps. Such Winning Match moments will strengthen the loyalty of your Game Changers as they feel not only respected and valued but also taken care of in their development.

Every Winning Match moment automatically creates the foundation for further Winning Match moments, when the implementation of a sparring session's result will later be reflected on by you and your Game Changers. As it is for top coaches and elite athletes, a match or competition doesn't end with a match point, crossing the finish line, or stepping up onto the podium to receive the winning trophy. It continues with key learnings after deep reflection and debriefing. Therefore, when you keep track of your sparring discussions, you have the basis for detailed discussions afterward so that you can reflect on what worked, why it worked, what didn't, and why, and with the answers contribute to the growth and development of your Game Changers.

THE ROLE OF CULTURE
FOR THE WINNING MATCH

I have shared with you how the Winning Match model and how Winning Match moments can be highly relevant and transformative in driving organizational success. Now imagine its impact, if it could be systematically scaled across an entire organization.

Some companies rely on rather outdated practices such as standardized and generic evaluations, schemes, rigid management and career programs, reactive hiring, or outsourced recruiting. I sometimes observe a latent culture of egalitarianism across organizations, where high-potential lists are drawn up based foremost on formal criteria like education, experience abroad, numbers of years in the company, or the performance assessment from the last year.

Culture always starts with leadership at the top, specifically with the senior leaders who model the behaviors they wish to see, decide who gets promoted, who gets a seat at the table, and what gets rewarded. Who is tasked with looking for those transformative individuals with the potential to make a true difference? Even when Game Changers are identified, structural inertia, like the idea that senior roles can only be given to those with a certain seniority or time with the company, can drive them away.

Add to this a reluctance to adequately reward impact. Even where performance pay exists, I sometimes see that it doesn't reflect the real value that Game Changers bring. And then: Why should they stay if their efforts go unrecognized in real terms, meaning compensation, stimulating projects, or the chance to advance?

Cultural change must start with leadership from the top, specifically leaders who model the behavior they wish to see: Who gets promoted, who gets a seat at the table, and what outcomes are rewarded. Talent identification and development is a strategic imperative, not just an initiative lead by Human Resources. I see this as a leadership imperative that requires deep personal commitment at the executive level.

My aspiration is that the Winning Match leadership model helps companies to better recognize and empower Game Changers. In my evaluation of over 600 categorized top talents, only a few met all the Game Changer criteria. Yet these rare individuals have been driving disproportionate value, results, outcomes, and success.

With clear criteria and a culture that promotes and values the extraordinary, companies and organizations can become unbeatable.

As an executive or senior leader, how can you now go about this? What are the important aspects to consider when bringing the Winning Match concept to your company? Think back on the Game Changer criteria (as introduced in Part I) as well as key competencies for Leadership Champions to engage intentionally with their Game Changers in productive and intensive sparring (as discussed in Part II). This provides the framework for everyone in a leadership position to further upskill and adapt their leadership. We have discussed the ways how, at the individual level, you can build Winning Match moments. Hopefully, by now, supporting and developing your Game Changers is firmly at the top of your personal leadership priority list.

To increase the impact, first start with your team. Encourage those who directly report to you to form Winning Match moments with their Game Changers. Lead by example, and take the time to get to know the Game Changers outside of your immediate environment, making yourself available to them as an additional sparring partner.

To drive even greater impact, you can look at what is

needed to catalyze change at an organizational level. First, decide on impactful ways to introduce the Winning Match leadership model to your most important leaders. Plan a kick-off meeting or dedicate time at an important summit or leadership meeting to look at the model as well as its concrete implementation. Share not just the framework of the Winning Match, but share some examples of how adopting this powerful model can make a difference to your team's performance and how that contributes to the company's performance overall.

For those of you already having a talent program, it will be imperative to make the distinction between the existing concept of talent and the very concrete characteristics of a Game Changer. This starts with building a common understanding of what makes Game Changers different, as well as what it takes to identify real Game Changers. When senior leadership is aligned on what defines a Game Changer, they can begin to understand what it takes to systematically identify and scout for those individuals who will really drive the business forward.

Based on this, there will be greater readiness to collectively explore how to use the Winning Match framework to have a broad organizational impact. This starts with identifying how to integrate the Winning Match concept into the leadership programs of your corporation, as well as

visibly promoting a culture of collectively-oriented ambition that is also focused on maximum generosity and the
desire to make a positive, lasting change in others.

To support successful implementation, it may be
necessary to evolve organizational systems and processes.
There may be resistance because all of these actions will
disrupt the status quo. So, you will need champions at the
highest levels to make it a reality. When I say disruptive,
I mean rejecting practices that promote underqualified
individuals, tolerate mediocrity, or protect order. It means
aligning salary, bonus, and incentive programs with the
Winning Match model so that Leadership Champions and
Game Changers get exceptional recognition. It means
that the organization does not pay strictly according
to position but rewards the definite added value that
a Winning Match creates for the company, and makes
the identification and promotion of Game Changers
by executives bonus-relevant. It creates ways for Game
Changers to access concrete development opportunities
in key positions, in order to keep them engaged and to
provide new challenges and greater visibility. If a manager
ignores their Game Changers, or if they staff their teams
on political considerations, rather than performance
and value creation, it should be reflected in their
performance appraisals.

And to reinforce the change, systematically and regularly communicate the benefits of the Winning Match performance culture to the entire company in an inspirational way. Highlight best practices, share success stories and role models. Develop a comprehensive campaign that includes personal sharing and testimonials that make it real and bring the concepts to life, moving from theory to practice to the visible bottom-line impact. Be creative in telling the story and communicating the message, using a variety of internal channels, especially social media, where others can add to the conversation and share their experience. Giving visibility to leaders who can explain the why and reinforce the Winning Match message will help the ideas land and inspire.

Evolving systems and processes take persistent input from senior leaders. But it has never been more important: Game Changers won't tolerate outdated management practices for long. They know their value, and they seek a different model of leadership. If their expectations don't match the kind of leadership that they seek, they might leave for better opportunities. Therefore, make Game Changer scouting and the development of Leadership Champions a top priority. In doing so, you will embed the values of the Winning Match leadership model deep into your organization and unlock its full potential.

EPILOGUE:
Beyond the Bottom Line

I have shared with you my personal story: My upbringing, the discovery of my passion for football, the realization of my talent for the game, my vision and ambition for success, and ultimately how that led to a professional sports career. I believe that with the support of a different kind of leadership, I would have been able to fulfill my dream as a professional athlete. Thankfully, however, the lessons I learned along the way led me to where I am today, and ultimately, to this book.

When I pivoted from professional sports to the study of performance psychology, I was blessed to receive a kind of support from both inside and outside academia that made a profound difference to me and my career path. Of course, I had put in the hard work to get my academic credentials and have taken the risks necessary to establish a successful consulting practice. However, I am well aware that along the way, there were Leadership Champions who cleared my path, offered their networks, sparred with me, and challenged my ideas. Ultimately, they offered themselves selflessly in service of my purpose and vision, encouraging my ideas and beliefs, even though many were untested and unconventional at the time.

Yet they didn't do this because it was their job to do so. They did it because they saw something in me that they felt could make a difference for others. Many years later, when I had the chance to speak to them again, they told me that, in their eyes, they felt that I was on a mission to do something game-changing. And instead of gate-keeping or seeing my work as a threat, those Leadership Champions actively encouraged and supported me.

The focus of this book has been the corporate world, and showing what is possible when companies can identify their Game Changers, people whose intellect, ideas, and energy can transform an organization from the inside out. Paired with the right kind of leadership—a Leadership Champion who recognizes their potential and value, supports their ambition, and clears the path—Game Changers generate outcomes that can outperform expectations and can reshape the future of the business.

After having collaborated with many CEOs, senior executives, and key decision-makers globally in some of the world's leading companies, and across various industries, such as pharmaceuticals, financial services, technology, infrastructure, entertainment, sports, tele-communications and information technology, aviation and transportation, agriculture, luxury goods, and science, I experienced firsthand that the Winning Match leadership model ultimately has the potential to have a massive positive impact on all businesses, including their top and bottom line. The Winning Match leadership model can help to increase growth and profits. It can maximize positive impacts for customers and clients. It can further create shareholder value. It can contribute to gaining market share and getting to the top ranking among competitors. But is that all? By far no. I believe that the Winning Match paradigm has the potential to be even more.

As you have seen throughout this book, making a difference for others, often through others, is very rewarding for me. So much so that in the last couple of years, I have significantly increased my time and efforts to engage in nonprofit activities, offering my knowledge, skills, and services for other good causes. Providing one's services in areas where the need is high, but the financial means are limited, can be deeply humbling. This has reinforced my conviction that leadership is ultimately about inspiring, guiding, and serving others, no matter the field.

What I observe with many of my clients is similar: Game Changers don't stop being Game Changers in only one area or field. And Leadership Champions don't stop leading when their workday ends. Many of them continue to foster positive change wherever they go. That means in their families, in their communities, and in society at large. And when they do, their impact multiplies.

While success in business and making a significant, meaningful, and valuable contribution to a company's achievements is an important fuel for many, it can also be applied to other areas of life and offer a deep and lasting sense of satisfaction across a lifetime. While corporate life offers opportunity, structure, and reward, many individuals, in the long term, at some point in their careers, start to look beyond quarterly results and the impact of their latest project or program. They start to ask not just: "What am I achieving in this company?" But "What am I contributing through this company and beyond?"

In that shift lies an additional powerful truth: The same game-changing mindset that drives innovation at work can be an engine for progress in the world. Game Changers who have mastered the art of delivering value, who are wired for solving complex problems and productively challenging the status quo, can bring that same energy to other causes that matter deeply to them beyond work.

I see this in many of the individuals that I coach. They are not just hungry to bring their innovative ideas to the executive team and into the boardroom. They see problems in their neighborhood, their community, and in the world around them, and they feel the responsibility to make positive change. And they find new and creative ways to do it.

Leadership Champions, too, can have a role far beyond organizational charts. They can demonstrate their leadership in the world outside of work, acting as mentors, sponsors, and connectors to others in areas and fields where it is needed. They can easily scout the people they see making a difference and support them in finding and following their purpose. Their leadership impact ripples through neighborhoods, networks, and all of the domains where they get involved.

I am personally inspired by the number of individuals whom I coach who aren't just fully committed Game Changers and Leadership Champions at work. After hours, they are volunteering in organizations having an impact, launching grassroots projects, using their entrepreneurial skills to build nonprofit organizations, foundations, mentoring start-up founders, and advising others trying something new for the benefit of other people. They raise money for causes they believe in. Their KPIs shift from company profit margins to lasting impact, from product launches to lives changed. Their success becomes measured not just by metrics, but by meaning.

When high-performing game-changing individuals take the initiative to serve a great cause, and when leaders stand behind them with trust and encouragement, this is where the Winning Match has its greatest power. When, for example, a senior leader shares their expertise with a nonprofit board or an individual with game-changing potential applies their skills to address inequality, health, or education gaps in their community, then the ripple effect of a Winning Match is real and lasting beyond the bottom line.

In the end, the Winning Match leadership model is more than the contribution to a winning corporate strategy. It is a way of thinking about people, potential, and purpose. It is a call to use your talent not only to succeed in business, but to serve others in the world. It's knowing that the drive and intelligence you acquired, built, and cultivated to achieve business success can also shape the world for the better.

This is my parting invitation and call to action: Now that you understand the power of a Winning Match, take this approach with you wherever you are and wherever your path may lead you. Keep the concepts close and use them for yourself, and to guide how you show up in your family, your community, in society, and in the world. Be a Leadership Champion and recognize the Game Changers around you. Support them. Believe in them. Encourage them. Be their sparring partner. And make them even better.

And just as importantly, continue to be a Game Changer yourself. Find the causes that stir your heart. Whether your impact is local or global, visible or behind the scenes, every effort matters. The world needs people who are willing to lead with purpose and act with courage to create better conditions and outcomes for others.

Because true top performance doesn't just change a company. It can change the world. There is still a lot to do.

LIST OF FIGURES

ACKNOWLEDGMENTS

We all need people who believe in us, who encourage us to think big, and who inspire us to forge our own path.

My sincere thanks to: Gianpietro Zappa, Rolf Wolfelsperger, Gerhard Steiner, John Salmela, Terry Orlick, Steve Johnson, Bernhard Segesser, Irene Wyss, Hanspeter Eisenhut, Guido Schilling, and Peter Carter.

To Leonardo and Tiziano: You are wonderful. You will each make it, in your own way. Count on me to always stand behind you. I am deeply grateful for our time together, for every magical moment, and for the way you let me see the world through your eyes.

And to Sabrina: I can't thank you enough. You are amazing. Your presence, love and strength have been incredible to me. With you by my side, everything has been so much better.

ABOUT THE AUTHOR

DR. CHRISTIAN MARCOLLI is a world-renowned expert in sustainable high performance. He is the founder and CEO of Marcolli Executive Excellence, a specialized, boutique-style management consulting firm that partners with Fortune 500 companies, C-suite executives, and leadership teams world-wide to deliver measurable, lasting success through elevated leadership impact, strategic focus, and mental toughness.

For more than two decades, Christian has coached senior executives, global brands, and elite athletes, helping them achieve and sustain extraordinary results. His clients include C-suite leaders from top global companies as well as sports icons, Olympic gold medalists, and world champions.

Christian's expertise lies at the intersection of psychology, leadership, and world-class performance, and is grounded in both academic rigor and real-world experience.

A former professional football player whose career was cut short by injury, Christian earned a PhD in applied psychology and specialized in performance psychology. He brings that same competitive drive and insight to his work as a performance coach and speaker.

In addition to his latest book, *Winning Match: Leadership for Game Changers*, Christian is the award-winning author of several leadership and business books. They include *The Melting Point, More Life, Please!, Teach Me Patience — NOW!, Equip Yourself To Be a Business Champion*, and two volumes of *Spotlight on Performance: Executive Inspiration*. He is also the co-author of the books by Olympic champions Dominique and Michelle Gisin.

Fluent in English, German, French, and Italian, Christian lives in Switzerland with his wife and their two sons. He delivers his programs globally, working in both English and German.

www.ingramcontent.com/pod-product-compliance
Lightning Source LLC
Chambersburg PA
CBHW040916210326
41597CB00030B/5092